7/5/13
$25.95

Rediscovering a Lost Freedom

Rediscovering
a Lost
Freedom

Rediscovering a Lost Freedom

The First Amendment Right to Censor Unwanted Speech

Patrick M. Garry

Transaction Publishers
New Brunswick (U.S.A.) and London (U.K.)

First paperback edition 2009

Copyright © 2006 by Transaction Publishers, New Brunswick, New Jersey.

All rights reserved under International and Pan-American Copyright Conventions. No part of this book may be reproduced or transmitted in any form or by any means, electronic or mechanical, including photocopy, recording, or any information storage and retrieval system, without prior permission in writing from the publisher. All inquiries should be addressed to Transaction Publishers, Rutgers—The State University, 35 Berrue Circle, Piscataway, New Jersey 08854-8042. www.transactionpub.com

This book is printed on acid-free paper that meets the American National Standard for Permanence of Paper for Printed Library Materials.

Library of Congress Catalog Number: 2005052989
ISBN: 978-0-7658-0322-1 (cloth); 978-1-4128-0860-6 (paper)
Printed in the United States of America

Library of Congress Cataloging-in-Publication Data

Garry, Patrick M.
    Rediscovering a lost freedom : the First Amendment right to censor unwanted speech / Patrick M. Garry.
              p. cm.
    Includes bibliographical references and index.
    ISBN 0-7658-0322-4 (cloth)
       1. Freedom of the press—United States. 2. Censorship—United States.
I. Title.

KF4775.G37   2006
342.7308'53—dc22

                                                              2005052989

For My Grandparents

Contents

Acknowledgments

Many of the theories presented in this book were developed in a series of articles previously published in various academic journals. Portions of this book were originally published in *SMU Law Review*, 57 SMU L. REV. 139 (2004) (reprinted with permission); *University of Pittsburgh Law Review*, 65 PITT. L. REV. 183 (2004) (reprinted with permission); *Michigan State Law Review*, 2004 MICH. ST. L. REV. 1 (2004) (reprinted with permission); *Nexus: A Journal of Opinion*, Vol. 10 (2005) (reprinted with permission); *San Diego Law Review*, 42 SAN DIEGO L. REV. 129 (2005) (reprinted with permission); and *Capital University Law Review*, 33 CAP. U. L. REV. 551 (2005) (reprinted with permission).

As with everything I have done since joining the faculty at the University of South Dakota School of Law, I could not have completed this book in the time and manner I did without the diligent, always reliable, and supremely competent advice and involvement of Candice Lerseth.

Introduction

In 2003, the Supreme Court handed down its much-awaited decision on the McCain-Feingold campaign finance bill. Among its provisions, the bill abolished "soft money" contributions to national party committees, placed limitations on fundraising by federal officeholders and candidates, and curtailed certain political advertisements from being televised within sixty days of a general election. Because it restricted the rights of people and groups to engage in various types of political speech, the law was challenged on First Amendment grounds. But, to the surprise of many, the Court in *McConnell v. Federal Election Commission*[1] upheld the bill—a bill that clearly exceeded the existing limits of First Amendment doctrine, as set forth in a series of post-Watergate judicial decisions.[2] In short, the Court's opinion in *McConnell*, which runs 298 pages, can be summed up in one phrase: changed circumstances.

Since the last major Supreme Court decision on campaign finance and political speech, circumstances were seen to have changed. The costs of political campaigns were spiraling. Fundraising scandals had plagued the Clinton presidency, and the appearance of corruption had reached crisis levels. The public was becoming exasperated by the role of money in politics. The integrity of the political process seemed more urgently in need of assistance than did the upholding of traditional free speech rights. Consequently, the McCain-Feingold bill was designed "to purge national politics" of the "pernicious influence of 'big money' campaign contributions."[3]

To accommodate these changed circumstances, the Court's doctrinal approach likewise changed. It approved of legislation that just several decades earlier would have been declared unconstitutional. Yet there was little objection to McCain-Feingold from the free-speech lobby. It quickly acquiesced, joining in the view that changed circumstances had necessitated a change in constitutional strictures.

Just three decades earlier, however, the Supreme Court had declared that the First Amendment "has its fullest and most urgent application precisely to the conduct of campaigns for political office."[4] Five years later, the *Buckley* decision overturned limitations on individual political expenditures, reasoning that such limitations restricted "political expression at the core of our electoral process and of the First Amendment freedoms."[5] Five years after that, the Court struck down an ordinance placing ceilings on contributions to certain political issue groups.[6] And as recently as 1996, the Court ruled unconstitutional various restrictions on the expenditures of political parties.[7]

In *Buckley*, the Supreme Court stated that the speech freedoms of one person could not be curtailed for the sake of leveling the political playing field. Similarly, in *First National Bank of Boston v. Bellotti*,[8] the Court rejected the "systemic corruption" argument as a rationale for restricting political speech. Nonetheless, by the time the McCain-Feingold bill came to the Court, changed circumstances had apparently dictated a shift in judicial doctrines. According to the Brennan Center for Justice, the bill was a necessary legal adjustment to "the most pressing of problems." But as the dissent in *McConnell* argued, the end result of the decision is that what was formerly the most protected of speech—political speech—now carried more restrictions than virtual child pornography, sexually explicit cable programming, tobacco advertising, and nude dancing.[9]

Just as with the demands to regulate political campaign speech, there have been escalating calls for new restrictions of indecent material appearing on radio, television, and the Internet. With respect to the latter, however, the courts have steadfastly opposed the imposition of any new restrictions. Even though changed circumstances have certainly occurred over the years in the quantity and quality of media content, the courts have resisted making the type of doctrinal adjustments to entertainment speech that were made in *McConnell v. FEC* regarding political speech. Indeed, over the past half-century, few areas of American life have changed to the degree that media content and pervasiveness have changed.

If changed circumstances can justify restrictions on the kind of speech that lies at the core of the First Amendment, then they should likewise justify regulations applying to the plethora of vile, vulgar, and violent entertainment speech increasingly filling the modern media. As one scholar notes, "American children are being exposed to violent entertainment at an alarming rate."[10] Violent and sexually explicit video games are marketed to children under the age of ten.[11]

Pornographic and hate-speech Internet sites can be accessed with just a click of the mouse. On the radio, which is perhaps the medium most available to young children, the "Opie & Anthony" show in New York broadcast a contest involving play-by-play descriptions of couples having sex in such public places as the zoo, a toy store, and St. Patrick's Cathedral; and the "Deminski & Doyle Show" in Detroit asked callers to be as graphic as they could when narrating their favorite sexual practices.[12]

Television is almost as bad. A research study found that in just the four years from 1998 to 2002, the use of profanity on television increased 95 percent during the so-called family hour time slot.[13] Even national rituals like the Super Bowl are no longer safe for general television audiences. Public outrage occurred after the 2004 Super Bowl halftime show in which singer Justin Timberlake tore away the clothing covering co-singer Janet Jackson's breast.[14] Later that same year, despite the uproar over the Jackson incident, a Cleveland news anchor appeared on television stripping out of her clothes to promote a story on public nudity.[15]

Another strikingly changed circumstance involving offensive media speech is its sheer prevalence. Those who wish to avoid violent and offensive speech can hardly do so, because it can appear anywhere and at anytime, with little advance warning. Using the seek key on the radio to find a station in an unfamiliar market may suddenly produce a shock-jock monologue on sexual deviance. Walking through the mall, past a music store, may expose the passerby to the crude and violent lyrics of a rap artist. Pop-up advertisements on the Internet can interrupt a child's research session with an invitation to join a sex chat line.

When the Supreme Court developed its current First Amendment doctrines, largely during the period from the 1950s to the 1970s, most of the controversies involved dissident political speech—for instance, socialists and communists trying to convey their radical agendas to a largely unreceptive public. But this is not the case with many of the current speech controversies. These disputes have very little to do with politics, even radical politics. Most controversial speech now comes in the form of entertainment programming being packaged and sold by large media corporations. Unlike the image often created by multi-millionaire entertainers seeking victim status, the conflicts are not connected with political issues or causes; they are not at all similar to the government crackdowns on suspected communists instigated by Senator Joseph McCarthy during the early 1950s. When an entertainer does come under scrutiny, as Howard Stern did from the Federal Communications Commission (FCC) during its increased vigilance following the Janet Jackson Super Bowl incident, he argues that he is being singled out for political reasons, punished for advocating views critical of the government. But anyone who has ever listened to Howard Stern knows that political commentary is not a primary purpose of his show.

This leads to yet another changed circumstance in today's communication marketplace. Not only is the entertainment speech more violent and indecent, but there is relatively much less political speech. During the eighteenth century, political news and commentary comprised over 90 percent of the content of newspapers—the only media at the time. Two and a half centuries later, the entertainment portion of media offerings has grown much faster and more pervasive than any political content, with the result that traditional news and social commentary is being increasingly crowded out of its space in the public attention.

As Oliver Wendell Holmes once wrote, "The life of the law has not been logic: it has been experience."[16] The Supreme Court's decision in *McConnell* reflects this pronouncement.[17] Because of "changed circumstances" in the reality of political campaigns, the Court reacted with a change in the legal doctrines governing political speech. Other constitutional rights have undergone similar changes. The Second Amendment right to bear arms has been curtailed because of the prevalence of guns and violence in America: An assault weapon ban was enacted into law, as were various gun registration requirements. The Fourth Amendment freedom from unreasonable search and seizure has been modified to allow law enforcement officials to conduct warrantless searches of homes if they suspect evidence is about to be destroyed or a crime committed. The Equal Protection prohibition against racial targeting has been altered so as to permit affirmative action programs aimed at assisting specific racial groups. Yet, despite all the changes in American's media environment, constitutional law has failed to adapt. The doctrines governing free speech remain virtually unchanged, stuck in an era preceding cable television and rap music and pornographic websites and shock-jock radio—stuck in an era in which the most controversial public speech was the political criticisms of socialists and pacifists.

In defending the McCain-Feingold bill, one of the attorneys argued that the Court should not construe the First Amendment as a straitjacket preventing Congress from addressing an urgent social problem. But this same argument could be made regarding speech that is much further from the core concern of the First Amendment—media entertainment that is filled with raw violence and gratuitous sex. Indeed, the rationales for protecting much of indecent speech no longer seem to fit, since they stem from a constitutional model that has become irrelevant and outmoded.

Current First Amendment doctrines are based on the marketplace model. This model strives to inject as much speech as possible into the public domain, to encourage the production of maximum amounts of speech. The underlying assumption of the marketplace model is that the competition of ideas will lead to the attainment of truth. The marketplace model, according to its defenders, offers a guide for how democratic society should govern itself. The magic formula is abundance. If the law is oriented to maximize the volume of speech, the natural functioning of the marketplace of ideas will work everything out; it will produce the truth and guidance that society needs; it will preserve the best ideas and discard all the useless and harmful ones.

Despite the criticisms levied here of the marketplace model, its historic successes cannot be denied. The United States is one of the most expressively open societies on earth, and its creative energies and accomplishments are the envy of the world. But the problem with the marketplace model is that the one thing of which there is no shortage in the modern world is volume of speech. Eighty-five percent of U.S. households, for instance, have cable or digital television capable of receiving hundreds of channels.[18] Another problem lies in the nature and source of the speech that does fill the media. The marketplace model envisions speech emanating from the "street corner speaker"—the idealized image of the eighteenth-century citizen voicing his political opinions in the town square. But in the twenty-first century, the overwhelming amount of public speech does not come from street corner speakers, even if the Internet has allowed for greater public participation in political dialogue. By far, most of the speech comes from media corporations. And instead of the political views of concerned street corner speakers, the vast majority of contemporary media speech is mere entertainment, which is essentially a mass-produced commodity, no different from a set of golf clubs or a new CD player.

Since most public speech is entertainment rather than political or informative, the controversies it generates are different from the controversies generated by street corner speakers. While the orator in the town square might anger government officials by his criticisms of tax policy or his demands for investigation of public corruption, the modern entertainer offends society by flouting whatever public decency standards remain. The subsequent controversy does not arise because of any government-initiated censorship of the speech, but because the average citizen is outraged by what their children see on television or listen to on the radio. And it is hardly an answer to that outrage to state that the only solution permitted by the First Amendment is to allow more speech, especially if that additional speech will only be more indecent or offensive entertainment.

If any speech is plentiful in America today, it is the speech of crudity, indecency, and violence. Under the First Amendment, indecency is accorded privileges not even given to religious speech. For instance, in *Santa Fe Independent School District v. Doe*,[19] the Court banned religious prayers from being recited over the public address system at high school football games, but in *Sable Communications, Inc. v. FCC*,[20] the Court overruled a congressional ban on pornographic prerecorded telephone messages, also known as "dial-a-porn" services.

For all practical purposes, the First Amendment has become monopolized by the media industry. It has become an insurmountable wall shielding entertainment companies from any accountability for the products they market. The First Amendment has become such an impenetrable shield that the media has become shameless in its hypocrisy. It condemns gun manufacturers for contributing to violence in America, even as it spews out entertainment content that glorifies raw, gratuitous violence. It seeks changes to the Second Amendment that would allow those gun manufacturers to be sued by victims of gun violence, even as it successfully resists any lawsuits by parents whose children have been victimized by aggressors acting under the influence of violent movies and video games. It preaches that the warning labels on cigarette cartons should not protect tobacco companies from liability, even as it evades and undermines its own largely ineffective rating system for video games, music lyrics, and television programming. It blames fast-food restaurants for causing obesity in America, even as it argues that any responsibility for indecent and violent forms of entertainment lie exclusively with parents who allow their children access to such entertainment.

Behind the shield of the First Amendment, Hollywood has been growing steadily more raw and aggressive in its entertainment programming. The courts' answer to this increasingly violent and sexually graphic programming is that offended viewers should simply "avert their eyes." This solution fits in perfectly with the marketplace model, since it does nothing to diminish the quantity of speech. It puts neither duties on the speaker nor any obstacles in the path of the speech. But this solution of averting one's eyes is completely disconnected from the realities of the modern media world. It is a solution that, because of the "changed circumstances" of the information age, has become unworkable.

Today, there is no way to erect a firewall between children and selected aspects of popular culture; the ubiquity of the media renders such personal selectivity nearly impossible. As Diana West observes, "Turning off your own TV set—or DVD player, or Internet connection—is a little like pulling the shade on one window of a large apartment building: The effect is zilch on where you live."[21] Even if the parents do not allow any video games in the house, there are plenty of arcades between home and school. Even if parents strictly monitor the television programs their children watch, there is absolutely no telling what kind of commercials will air during those programs; nor will parents be able to monitor all the public venues where large video screens will be tuned into MTV, with its singers more absorbed in simulating sex than in mouthing the lyrics to a song. Moreover, the difficulty of monitoring a child's media exposure is exponentially magnified if both parents are working, or if the household is run by a single parent (notwithstanding Hollywood's glorification of single parenthood).

Much of contemporary entertainment is designed precisely to prevent any "averting of eyes." There is a reason children sit so motionlessly in front of the television, and why they unthinkingly echo the words of a song, and why their eyes become so glued to video games. The reason is that these forms of entertainment, unlike the "street corner speaker," aim not to logically engage but to psychologically capture. They seek not to inspire debate, but to prompt an addiction. Expecting people to constantly avert their eyes from so much of popular entertainment, which is designed to appeal to the addictive vulnerabilities of people, is like leaving a bowl of candy sitting out on the table and somehow expecting sweet-toothed children to "avert their eyes" (and stomachs).

The courts place all the burdens of monitoring offensive and harmful entertainment on the listener and viewer, even after the media has invested millions of dollars to make their entertainment products addicting and unavoidable. History has shown that human beings have a weakness, a vulnerable attraction, to instinctual urges toward sex and violence. Up until recent times, the human saga has been a story of people trying to control those urges and temptations. Whole cultures of civilized practices were built up over centuries to control such urges and temptations. But this centuries-long effort is being quashed by the modern media's pervasive exploitation of sex and violence.

The unrealistic expectation that people should simply avert their eyes might be more palatable if the speech from which eyes had to be averted qualified as speech necessary or even helpful to democratic governance. There would be stronger justification for keeping unpopular speech front-and-center if it concerned advocacy of an unwanted war or the raising of opposed taxes or the continuation of a discredited juvenile justice program. But this is not what the vast majority of media entertainment is all about. In fact, the vast majority of media entertainment has no such social significance or importance. It is simply like the candy bar that sits out on the table: It simply can't be avoided.

The marketplace model's assumption that "good" speech can only be assured through the protection of "bad" speech has come under question during the current era of abundant speech. Disillusion with the marketplace model has occurred even with many liberals, who have long been some of the strongest supporters of free speech. The continued existence of hate-speech, which can sabotage racial harmony, and pornographic speech, which feminists claim objectifies women, have prompted liberals to modify their positions on what speech should be protected and how it should be protected. Some even go so far as to advocate direct government intervention in the communications process. Reformers like Professor Cass Sunstein argue that government should actively regulate the media, even with content-specific mandates, so as to achieve a more healthy and constructive political dialogue; they say that government should intervene if people's private speech decisions do not foster sufficient political deliberation and diversity of ideas.[22] Citing "changed circumstances" insofar as the sexism and racism of the past can no longer be tolerated, these interventionists question why speech that has such a detrimental effect on society should be constitutionally immune from any democratic reform. As Sunstein writes, First Amendment protections are now "giving the name freedoms to the most flagrant enslavements of our minds and wills."[23]

This diminished support for free speech protection, according to Steven Gey, suggests the arrival of a "First Amendment legal realism," coming some "seventy years after its appearance in other areas of law."[24] Unlike the marketplace view of abundant speech as an automatic precursor to social truth, legal realism takes a more skeptical view of the realities of the modern media world. It sees the absolute and unwavering protection of all speech as a hindrance to achieving other social goals, such as fairness, equality, and justice. With such attitudes, however, the danger is that a sweeping backlash against free speech freedoms may occur. If nothing is done to address some of the most harmful speech elements existing today, as well as the relative helplessness of individuals to counteract the pervasive presence of media speech, the First Amendment may face even greater challenges in the future.[25]

The state-action proposals articulated by free speech reformers like Cass Sunstein raise their own set of alarms. Direct government regulation of the content of speech, especially political speech, has taken centuries to eliminate. History has also shown that a "responsible press" cannot be legislated into existence, even though growing numbers of legal scholars believe that a dysfunctional media so disserves the public interest that government intervention is warranted. Moreover, there is no guarantee that political factions will not use their temporary power to try to permanently silence their opponents. The question then becomes: If direct government intervention in the communications marketplace is unacceptable, what else can be done? The answer may lie at the very heart of the First Amendment: the notion of individual control over his or her communications process.

In First Amendment terms, the issue of individual control currently prevailing is not the one that existed during the 1950s or the World War I era. The current issue is not the individual's right to speak as she pleases (there is virtually nothing that individuals cannot say, aside from shouting "bomb" in a crowded airport); nor is the issue one of an individual's right to obtain speech—not only is speech plentiful, but there is a vast array of different sources for each type of speech sought. Instead, the one issue of individual control that is most in need of addressing is the issue of how individuals can avoid having themselves and their children bombarded with speech they consider degrading and destructive. As argued above, this control cannot realistically be achieved through simply averting one's eyes. Nor should individuals in the modern information age be forced into an all-or-nothing position. They should not have to unplug the television or disconnect the Internet just because they wish to avoid graphic violence and lurid sexuality. Such an approach would certainly not help to build a citizenry engaged in the modern world.

No one claims that the First Amendment should require someone to listen to a speech she does not want to hear, nor view a program she does not want to watch, nor subscribe to a newspaper she finds distasteful. And yet, because of the pervasiveness of the modern media and the concerted attempt by an entire industry to "hook" the American public on certain types of entertainment, individuals may not be able to so easily draw away from speech that their rational minds tell them they should avoid. Individuals may need help regaining some semblance of control in a media-saturated society, especially as the media slides further and further into the peddling of degradation. But as long as this control rests in the individual, even if facilitated by some governmental assistance, and as long as there is not a complete denial of speech to desiring listeners or viewers, then nothing in the First Amendment should prevent such control from being possessed.

The First Amendment states that speech shall not be repressed by the government. This means that the government cannot stop people from speaking; nor can it prevent people's speech from reaching a willing audience. Over the past four decades, however, courts have employed the marketplace model to craft an overly expansive view of the First Amendment speech clause. They have interpreted the clause to mean not just that the speaker be free, but that her speech must flow to every corner of the social marketplace without any diversions whatsoever. The courts have ruled free speech to mean that any listener or viewer must be able to access that speech without any inconveniences or burdens. But this was not how speech operated during the constitutional period. Back then, people had to make great efforts to obtain news and opinion. They had to gather in the cold and rain as an orator spoke in the town square; they had to walk to a public house to read one of the few copies of a newspaper. In the modern age, however, the presumption is that speech must flow to every potential listener with barely an ounce of effort exerted by that listener. Of course, this approach has led to a problem unthinkable in the eighteenth century—the problem of listeners being deluged with speech they do not want and cannot seem to avoid.

The last thing someone does during a flood is to water the lawn, but that has been the judicial response to the flooding of violent and sexual speech that the media age has brought. There have been regulatory stabs made at this problem, but they have not succeeded. Ratings have been placed on gruesomely violent video games, but the manufacturers still market the games to young children and the stores still sell them. The FCC has been charged with enforcing decency standards on broadcast radio and television, but the current state of programming on those media testify as to the lack of success the agency has had.

Although government regulation has not succeeded, a more workable solution might lie in giving the individual greater control to do his or her own censoring of media content. What might be the answer is to return to individuals the power they possessed two hundred years ago: the power to reject intrusive and offensive speech.

Speech means more than words flying out of someone's mouth. Fundamentally, speech is a process of communication. But communication is a two-way street. The listener is as much a part of the process as is the speaker. Consequently, for the courts to focus their First Amendment doctrines strictly on the speaker or the sheer volume of speech is to ignore the whole other side of the equation.

Given the realities of the modern world, most people will never publish op-ed pieces in newspapers or host their own political talk show on television. For most people, their speech acts will involve selecting, and rejecting, those ideas or expressions with which they agree or disagree. In the modern world, censorship is the speech of the inarticulate—and for them to have expressive freedom, they should be free to reject certain unwanted speech and to disassociate themselves and their families from what they consider socially or morally repulsive speech. Given the flood of media speech that exists in the modern world, individuals should be able to privately and effectively censor that speech. Given the changed circumstances that have developed in the media world, the First Amendment should be interpreted to recognize such a private right of censorship.

The past several decades have witnessed a "rights explosion." Under the First Amendment, there is a right to speak, a right not to speak, and a right to listen. The only remaining right is the right not to listen. It is a right made necessary by the realities of the information world. It is a right that seeks to expand the amount of control possessed by all the individuals who have been rendered increasingly passive by the overwhelming pervasiveness of the modern media. In seeking to give the listener more power, a private right to censor may place diversions in the path of certain speech; it may mean that the speaker does not have absolute control over all the destinations of her speech; it may mean that willing listeners will have to make some effort to receive all the different kinds of speech they desire. But a private right to censor will not overrule the right of speech. It will not shut down speech or silence speakers: It will simply give listeners some individual control amidst the growing tide of speech that washes in on them every day of their lives.

This book will set out the parameters of the proposed private right to censor. It will draw together the case law that has already laid a foundation for this right, and it will examine the ways in which the government can act to help facilitate such a right. It will analyze how a private right to censor could be implemented. Attempting to return to the original intent of the First Amendment, a distinction will be made between political speech necessary for the conduct of self-government and non-political speech that serves merely to entertain or advertise. Only in connection with non-political speech will the private right to censor be applied.

Without question, the theory underlying such a right envisions the possibility of government action that would help empower viewers and listeners, and without question such government action would make some non-political speech less convenient and accessible than it is now. But that speech would still be available; it would not be silenced or totally cut-off.

If the Supreme Court in *McConnell v. FEC* is right, changed circumstances should allow a democratic society some leeway in shaping its constitutional commands. There should be some freedom of experimentation accorded to democratic legislatures to address pressing social problems. Such freedom may now be necessary in connection with the increasingly harmful types of entertainment to which children are being exposed. Modern society may have reached the point where the presumption underlying the marketplace model must finally be put to the test: Does all the "bad" speech have to be protected so as to keep the "good"? And is the First Amendment a straitjacket that confines us to a media world of venality, vulgarity, and violence?

As former FCC chairman Newton Minow observes, "If we accept the notion that the First Amendment prohibits us from trying to protect our children from the mass media, we have committed the perverse error of divorcing our commitment to free speech—the gift by which the Founding Fathers intended us to deliberate on the public interest—from our commitment to the public interest itself."[26] Since the ratification of the First Amendment, there has been a sea change in American life: from individuals relatively isolated from vulgar and indecent speech, to individuals besieged with such speech. Perhaps the only effective yet constitutional response to this change is to recognize within the First Amendment a private right to censor.

Notes

1.   *McConnell v. Federal Election Com'n*, 124 S. Ct. 619 (2003).
2.   Perhaps the most important of these is *Buckley v. Valeo*, 424 U.S. 1 (1976).
3.   *McConnell*, 124 S. Ct. 619, 644 (2003).
4.   *Monitor Patriot Co. v. Roy*, 401 U.S. 265, 272 (1971).
5.   *Buckley*, 424 U.S. 1, 39 (1976).
6.   *Citizens Against Rent Control v. City of Berkeley*, 454 U.S. 290 (1981).
7.   *Colorado Republican Federal Campaign Committee v. Federal Election Com'n*, 518 U.S. 604 (1996).
8.   *First National Bank of Boston v. Bellotti*, 435 U.S. 765 (1978).
9.   *McConnell*, 124 S. Ct. 619, 720.
10.   Emily R. Caron, "Blood, Guts & The First Amendment," 11 *Kansas Journal of Law & Public Policy*, 89, 91 (2001).
11.   Joseph Pereira, "Games Get More Explicit," *Wall Street Journal*, September 25, 2003, D1.
12.   Matthew Quirk, "Air Pollution," *Atlantic Monthly*, May 2004, 36.
13.   Joel Timmer, "The Seven Dirty Words You Can Say on Cable and DBS," 10 *Communications Law & Policy* 179, 182 (2005).
14.   Theresa Chidester, "What the #$ is Happening on Television?" 13 *CommLaw Conspectus* 135, 156 (2004).
15.   David Carr, "When a TV Talking Head Becomes a Talking Body," *New York Times*, November 25, 2004, B1.
16.   Oliver Wendell Holmes, Jr., *The Common Law* (Boston: Little, Brown, and Company, 1881), 1.
17.   Although I cite the *McConnell* case for its reflection of the "changed circumstances" rule, I offer no opinion here as to the substance or reasoning of the opinion.
18.   Christopher Yoo, "The Rise and Demise of the Technology-Specific Approach to the First Amendment," 91 *Georgetown Law Journal* 245, 345 (2003).
19.   *Carter v. United States*, 530 U.S. 271 (2000).
20.   *Sable Communications of California, Inc. v. F.C.C.*, 492 U.S. 115 (1989).

14   **Rediscovering a Lost Freedom**

21. Diana West, "All That Trash," *Public Interest*, Summer 2004, 131.
22. Cass Sunstein, "Free Speech Now," 59 *University of Chicago Law Review* 255, 289 (1992).
23. Ibid., 255.
24. Steven Gey, "The Case Against Postmodern Censorship Theory," 145 *University of Pennsylvania Law Review* 194 (1996).
25. G. Edward White, "The First Amendment Comes of Age: The Emergence of Free Speech in Twentieth-Century America," 95 *Michigan Law Review* 299, 310 (1996).
26. West, "All That Trash," 131.

1

The Outdated Arguments Used to Defend Modern Media Speech

The Modern Media and the Transformation of Speech

In 1919, *Schenck v. United States* presented the Supreme Court its first opportunity to interpret and apply the First Amendment.[1] The case marked the first time in the Court's 130-history that anyone attempted to use the First Amendment as a shield against government prosecution, and it was the first time the Court evaluated federal legislation in connection with the right of free speech. *Schenck* involved an appeal from a conviction of socialists who, in violation of the Espionage Act, had circulated antiwar leaflets urging men to resist being drafted into the military. The Court upheld the conviction, ruling that the leaflets created a clear and present danger to the nation's military recruitment during a time of war.

Throughout the decades following *Schenck*, First Amendment speech cases continued to arrive at the Court. With the start of the Cold War and the American standoff against the Soviet Union, laws were passed that specifically targeted the speech freedoms of communist activists in the United States. In *Dennis v. United States*,[2] the Court sustained these laws, finding that Communist party leaders advocating overthrow of the U.S. government posed a clear and present danger of the kind Congress was empowered to regulate.

Eventually, however, the tide started turning. In the 1957 case of *Yates v. United States*,[3] the Court ruled in favor of free speech rights, overturning the Smith Act convictions of fourteen "lower-echelon" Communist party members. Similar rulings occurred in *Aptheker v. Secretary of State*,[4] *Noto v. United States*,[5] and *United States v. Robel*.[6] These rulings reflected the growing influence of the marketplace argument:

that a democratic government could survive only if its prevailing "truth" was continually questioned by dissident views. This argument became the foundation from which sprang the free speech revolution of the 1960s.

By 1969, the Court had moved firmly into the free speech corner, never again to budge.[7] Underlying this shift was the realization that political disagreement was vital to a democracy as diverse as America's. If robust political debate was to occur, the government could not make preconceived judgments about which speech would be heard and which would not. A vibrant democracy could not exist if whole groups of people and viewpoints were excluded from the political discourse.

Operating under these assumptions, the Court began granting full constitutional protection to speech that, as time progressed, steadily drifted away from the kind of speech at issue in *Schenck* and *Dennis* and *Yates*. In *Cohen v. California*,[8] the Court ruled that the words "Fuck the Draft," printed on a jacket worn by a young man as he walked through a crowded courthouse, qualified for constitutional protection. Even though the message contained a vulgarity offensive to many who viewed it, the Court held it to be a protected viewpoint. Later, in *Barnes v. Glen Theatre, Inc.*,[9] the Court recognized that nude dancing was a form of protected expression. In *Hustler Magazine v. Falwell*, it ruled that a cartoon depicting a well-known religious leader in a drunken incestuous rendezvous with his mother in an outhouse qualified for First Amendment protection.[10] More recently, in *Ashcroft v. ACLU*, the Court struck down a congressional statute that attempted to prohibit certain types of "virtual" child pornography.[11]

Perhaps the most significant difference between the free speech cases heard by the courts prior to 1970 from those after 1970 is that the former tended to involve political speech expressing specific political ideologies, whereas the latter tends to involve vulgar or sexually explicit speech. Whereas the former group involved individuals trying to convert people to an unpopular political creed, the latter involve speech that is part of an entertainment-for-profit endeavor. As Professor Sunstein notes, although the major First Amendment suits in the 1940s, 1950s, and 1960s were brought by political dissidents, many of the current cases involve complaints by commercial entertainment distributors.[12] Nonetheless, this entertainment speech has availed itself of all those First Amendment doctrines developed to protect the inclusion of dissident voices in the nation's political discourse.

The vast majority of current free speech disputes involve entertainment speech that is accused of being graphically violent or sexually explicit. Public complaints of broadcast indecency have skyrocketed. The FCC Consumer and Governmental Affairs Bureau reported a "huge increase" in such complaints in 2003.[13] The entertainment industry tells viewers that the solution to unwanted offensive speech is not to watch it, to "avert one's eyes" from it. But this presumes that the public knows in advance when and where such speech will occur. As evidenced by the 2004 Super Bowl halftime show, such predictability is no longer possible. People cannot even watch the nation's premier sporting event without being exposed to images they do not want their children to see. As *TIME* magazine observes, from the unwanted porn email to the "hamburger commercial with a woman lasciviously riding a mechanical bull," people today "feel mugged by pop culture."[14] Cable television, the pop music industry, the Internet, and video games are all "expanding the reach and depths of the media cesspool exponentially."[15] As the executive secretary of the Iowa Freedom of Information Council notes, American children "are swimming around in this pop culture that is becoming a sort of sewer."[16]

Because so many of the current speech controversies involve violent or indecent entertainment programming, the instigator of most attempted censorship measures is not the government, as it was during the censorship regimes of the 1920s and 1950s, but members of the outraged public. In the area of censorship, the government has backed away from the forefront, reacting to public complaints only when the political pressure rises to a point where it cannot be ignored, as it did following the 2004 Super Bowl. If anything, government has become a most reluctant censor. Of the thousands of indecency complaints received each year, the FCC imposes sanctions on only a minuscule number of offenders.

Critics overwhelmingly agree that broadcast programming is engaged in a "race to the bottom." As Woody Allen once said, "In Beverly Hills, they don't throw their garbage away; they make it into television shows."[17] The rash of "reality shows" on television is particularly reflective of this free-fall from any artistic or decency standards. On "Family Bonds," viewers were exposed to one family's most intimate moments: from the mother listing how many times a night she has sex, to a live shot of the older sister giving birth.[18] An episode of "Married By America" featured strippers covered in whipped cream.[19] The housemates on "Real World" performed "three-ways" in hot tubs. And in "Amish in the City," a series in which five youths raised as Amish were exposed on camera to all the temptations of the fast life in L.A., the producers deliberately appealed to the audience's prurient interest in seeing these young people violate and abandon the most basic beliefs with which they were raised.[20]

Not only do its reality shows appeal to the lowest instincts of viewers, but its increasingly violent and sexually explicit programming is celebrated by the entertainment world. In 1996, critics applauded a film about the First Amendment crusades of Larry Flynt, whose magazine *Hustler* features "drawings of women bound, tortured, and crawling with maggots."[21] That same year, Hollywood flocked to the defense of *Cannibal Corpse*—a group whose song "Necroebophile" describes, among other things, masturbating with the severed head of a child.

The Extremism and Irrelevance of Many Free Speech Defenses

When radio shock jock Howard Stern was fined by the FCC for on-air statements about anal sex and other sexual activities, he accused the government of conducting a "McCarthy-type witch hunt" because of criticisms he had made of President Bush.[22] Stern compared the FCC fine to "Nazi-era censorship."[23] This has become a popular tactic of broadcast entertainers sanctioned for their vulgar and indecent speech: to recharacterize their talk of graphic and often bizarre sexuality as an expression of political viewpoints. Entertainers have also taken to describing any public opposition to their opinions as repressive, unconstitutional censorship. A *Los Angeles Times* media critic said that when a Las Vegas audience walked out on singer Linda Ronstadt's anti-American tirade during a performance, "the most fundamental of liberties came under assault."[24] By so characterizing themselves as victims of social censorship, these entertainers can put forward all the defenses formerly asserted by America's political minorities, like the socialist in *Schenck* and the communist in *Dennis* who sought the freedom to participate in the nation's democratic processes.

One of the most common free speech defenses is the slippery-slope argument, which states that any constraint on any type of speech will inevitably lead down a slippery slope to an eventual loss of all freedoms, that any deviation from the absolute protection of even the most revolting speech will lead down a slippery slope to tyranny, that the Inquisition is just one exception away. This is the helpless-judge argument, reflecting the belief that judges are helpless to make sound and reasoned distinctions. They are helpless to distinguish between a James Joyce novel and a Howard Stern monologue on lesbian sex. But if judges are so incapable of making such judgments, why have they been given the power of judicial review? If they cannot make distinctions between the trash-talk of a Howard Stern radio show and the philosophical explorations of one of the twentieth century's greatest literary novelists, then they surely cannot decide which laws passed by democratic legislatures pass constitutional muster. If judges are constrained from acting, lest they slide helplessly down the slippery slope to chaos, then they are no better than preprogrammed machines rigidly performing a predictable procedure.

The second defense commonly asserted in free speech disputes is the truth defense. Truth, it is argued, will naturally result from the competitive interaction of the maximum number of ideas.[25] This is the "invisible hand" theory—that abundant speech will lead automatically to truth. By definition, the theory is self-fulfilling, because its advocates simply define truth "as that which survives the process."[26] Truth is simply assumed to flow from sufficiently voluminous speech.[27]

Although this truth argument was perfectly appropriate when it was first advanced in the early part of the twentieth century, it is not as relevant in the media-saturated world of the twenty-first century. It now seems riddled with inconsistencies and contradictions. Indeed, no one has ever been able to prove what valuable truth has been produced by pornography of the type that appears in Larry Flynt's *Hustler* magazine. Nor is there any "truth" value in speech that society has firmly rejected after centuries of struggle—for example, "truths" like racial hate. Furthermore, it is a dangerous omen for the future of human society if "truth" now derives from violent video games and vulgar music lyrics. It seems a great step backward if two hundred years ago "truth" came from educated debate and the study of history's great philosophers, whereas now it results from mindlessly watching music videos. If entertainment rather than intellectual study is the source of truth, then perhaps the whole notion of truth has become corrupted; when "entertaining" is seen as equivalent to "informing," then perhaps truth has eroded into relativistic ambiguity. Indeed, there are many in our skeptical age who deny any validity at all to the notion of truth. The deconstructionists and multiculturalists argue that "truth" is an illusion, nothing more than the artificial construct of racial and gender power struggles in society. To them, objective truth does not exist.

Even among those who do argue that truth results from a competition of the maximum amount of speech, many nonetheless refuse certain parties the right to participate in that competition. When in 1997 the Vatican issued a report titled "Ethics in Advertising," denouncing the advertising practices in Western societies, media spokespersons criticized the Church for trying to dictate content. The free enterprise system provided its own policing, the argument went: The Vatican "should stick to religion, and we'll stick to advertising."[28]

A third defense of unrestricted speech freedoms involves the process of self-government.[29] This defense sees the practice of democracy as originating with robust debate and democratic dialogue, arising out of voluminous speech in the public domain. Advocates of this defense, however, have difficulty in explaining why violent video games and television dating shows, none of which have much to do with political deliberation or self-governance, should be protected by the First Amendment.[30] Furthermore, the assumption that voluminous speech necessarily produces the rational ideas needed for self-governance flies in the face of the fact that the great majority (and the fastest-growing component) of media speech is no more than an entertainment commodity, designed not to be rational but addictive. As Sunstein notes, "The production of most television shows is not a contribution to democratic deliberation or even a means of self-expression, but instead a fairly ordinary business decision for which the First Amendment was not designed to provide protection."[31]

Proponents of the self-governance defense are also hard pressed to explain why political engagement has declined even as media speech has exploded. Indeed, an inverse relationship has developed in this regard. According to studies, the younger generation "knows less, cares less, and votes less than young people at any time during the past half century."[32] Robert Putnam, author of *Bowling Alone*, reports that voter turnout fell by nearly 25 percent between the early 1960s and the late 1990s. Roper Organization surveys have revealed that the number of Americans who attended community meetings and political rallies declined 50 percent from 1973 to 1993. As Putnam notes: "By almost every measure, Americans' direct engagement in politics and government has fallen steadily and sharply." It is almost as if the information age and media explosion has had the reverse effect, undermining democratic involvement and making individuals feel more powerless and more disconnected in the modern media world.

Another free speech defense is the safety valve defense. According to this defense, free speech provides a safety valve for all of society's pent-up urges toward violence and crudity; for without a totally open system of free-flowing speech, those urges would fester, until exploding as full-scale violence. But rather than venting an occasional urge toward antisocial behavior, contemporary media speech seems to have incorporated the most gruesome violence as a routine experience. Contrary to the safety-valve theory, as society's speech has become more violent so too has its actions. Instead of being a vent for instinctual urges toward violence, media content seems to be instigating the violence. Television programming has become so violent since the 1970s that no serious researcher disputes the notion that overexposure to television violence can help transform children into violent adults.[33] Twenty years after the U.S. Surgeon General in 1972 postulated a link between watching televised violence as a child and engaging in violent behavior as an adult, the *Journal of the American Medical Association* published the first epidemiological study linking exposure to television violence to the subsequent commission of violent crimes. Research has found "a strong correlation between the exposure of children to televised violence and a number of behavioral and psychological problems."[34]

The argument is also made that censorship will cause the social communications system to "reflect only the views of a small privileged minority."[35] However, without any ability of the public to censor, then the social communications system will reflect only the views of the Hollywood and media elite.

Perhaps the reason all these speech defenses have lost their force is that they all stem from the marketplace model, and in the current media world this model has become inapplicable. Indeed, all the assumptions incorporated into the marketplace model are teetering on the edge of irrelevance.

The Role of the Marketplace Model
in First Amendment Jurisprudence

According to the marketplace model, a sufficient quantity of speech will naturally lead to a sufficient quality. The model envisions a situation resembling the workings of an Adam Smith economy, where an unhindered supply of speech will produce a perfect competition among ideas. This competition will ideally lead to truth, which in turn will lead to rational and enlightened self-government. No concern is put on the content or character of the speech involved, since such determinations are left up to the marketplace.

Incorporated within this model is the assumption that "good" speech will eventually choke out the "bad" (yet in reality, just the opposite is occurring).[36] So confident is the model in this assumption that it even welcomes and encourages the entrance of "bad" ideas, since only by competing against these can the worthiness of "good" ideas be established. Consequently, even the most innocuous of regulations, if they create distinctions or burdens based on content, will likely be struck down.[37] In the political speech arena, at least up until the *McConnell* decision, the Court has repeatedly focused on quantity rather than quality, and has overturned laws that in any way decrease the amount of speech existing in the electoral process.[38] Indeed, under the marketplace model, indecent and violent speech is protected as soundly as are political editorials.[39]

Over the years, the marketplace model has proved to be the dominant one employed in the Court's free speech jurisprudence—the model most used to decide First Amendment controversies.[40] According to one legal scholar, the marketplace model "has dominated recent First Amendment discourse."[41] Therefore, when the interests of willing or potentially willing listeners conflict with the interests of unwilling listeners, the former will almost always prevail in any constitutional analysis, no matter how few in number the willing listeners may be as compared to the unwilling.[42]The marketplace of ideas metaphor was first expressed by Justice Holmes in his famous dissent in *Abrams v. United States*.[43] This view of free speech—that an open marketplace of competing ideas will lead to the discovery of truth—had already been outlined in the early theories of John Milton and John Stuart Mill.[44] But the real accomplishment of Holmes was to elevate free speech above that of merely an individual interest, which was unlikely to prevail when balanced against important social interests.

In his *Abrams* dissent, Holmes borrowed from the free speech theories of Zechariah Chafee, who argued that the true meaning of freedom of speech lay in its contribution to democratic society.[45] According to Chafee, the discovery and spread of truth on subjects of public interest constituted one of the most important purposes of society and government, and such discovery was only possible through free and unlimited discussion. This theory gave Holmes a greater rationale than just individual freedom for protecting speech. No longer should speech be protected only because individuals should be free to say and do whatever they liked; free speech should be protected because it was necessary for the survival of democracy. Under this view, free speech could then weigh more heavily on the judicial balance with other social interests such as national security.

In *Abrams*, the Court upheld the Sedition Act convictions of individuals who had distributed pamphlets calling for a general strike to protest the government's expeditionary force to Russia. Holmes' dissent relied on the marketplace of ideas metaphor—the argument that "the best test of truth is the power of the thought to get itself accepted in the competition of the market." This marketplace metaphor would eventually exert a profound impact on First Amendment law. Judicial opinions in the latter part of the twentieth century generally adopted the view of the First Amendment as set forth in the *Abrams* dissent.[46]

Despite its influence on the development of First Amendment doctrine, however, the role of the marketplace model has changed in recent decades, especially as the majority of speech cases have come to involve sexually explicit forms of entertainment rather than the more traditional forms of political dissent. Whereas the model used to rely ultimately on the quality of speech—namely, the achievement of truth—now it looks only to the quantity of speech, with little pretext at serving any larger cause. Now the marketplace model is not so much a rationale for protecting speech as it is a simple descriptor for how the law actually works—for instance, protecting as much speech as can be crammed into the media marketplace.

Ever since Holmes's articulation of it in 1919, the marketplace model has advocated maximizing the amount of speech in the system. The issue some eight decades later is whether, under the doctrine of "changed circumstances," a different view of the First Amendment is needed for the survival of a culture on which self-government depends.

A host of "changed circumstances" have eroded many of the underlying conditions of the marketplace metaphor. In Holmes' view, all ideas would enter the marketplace on an equal footing, by way of the "street corner speaker." But in the modern world, the sources of speech are a far cry from the "poor and puny anonymities" of Holmes' marketplace of ideas.[47] The "speakers" in the contemporary marketplace of ideas are media conglomerates that tend to see the public as a mere commodity, an audience to be delivered up to advertisers. And to attract as large an audience as possible, the media designs entertainment programming that is aimed at the lowest common denominator.[48] In today's world, the "ideas" that get injected into the marketplace are backed by millions of dollars of marketing power. Sensational ads lure kids into the latest video games; seductive images entice purchases of musical recordings; elaborate marketing campaigns push the latest television programs.

In the world of Holmes's marketplace of ideas, no individual speaker played a dominant role. An equality of power existed among all potential speakers, and listeners could freely choose when to participate in the communications marketplace and when to remove themselves from it. But this equality does not exist today, in a communications marketplace dominated by the entertainment industry.

Applying the marketplace model to the current media environment is like watering the lawn during a downpour. The grass isn't being watered; it's being washed away. The singular focus on breaking down any and all inconveniences that potential listeners might encounter in the process of accessing even the most disgusting speech is turning the whole media system against the moral and cultural interests of a democratic society. Contrary to the original conditions underlying the abundance assumption, it is now easier to access speech than avoid it. It is far easier to expose children to violent and sexually explicit material than it is to shield them from such speech. Thus the vulnerability of listeners and viewers in the modern world is a "changed circumstance" to which First Amendment doctrines should adjust.

The Eroding Relevance of the Marketplace Model

The one accomplishment of which the marketplace model can certainly boast is that of increasing the sheer volume of speech. The number of broadcast television stations that the average U.S. household can receive has more than tripled over the last twenty years.[49]

Moreover, cable television and direct broadcast satellite systems, which are now almost universally available, can provide hundreds of additional channels. Then there are personal video recorders and wireless local area networks and other emerging spread-spectrum technologies, as well as packet-switched networks, all of which will further increase the sources of speech. The FCC acknowledged this explosion in information sources as far back as 1987 when it eliminated the Fairness Doctrine.[50] But this explosion in numbers of sources has not transformed the media into an Adam Smith type of marketplace in which truth always prevails.

Under the marketplace model, there is no effective solution to the enormous volume of ugly and offensive speech. The models simply asserts that in its public debate society "must tolerate insulting, and even outrageous, speech in order to provide adequate breathing space to the freedoms protected by the First Amendment."[51] But this presumes that a public debate is occurring, that the "speech" in the public domain is even capable of debate, that this "speech" is more than mere images meant to manipulate emotions rather than contribute to some rational discussion, and that music videos are as communicative in a First Amendment sense as newspaper editorials. But music videos are not debating partners, nor do they even allow for countervailing debate. A music video does not include space at the end of the video for opponents to state their case. A video game does not give equal time to critics to make their point. Music videos and video games are monopolistic media: They allow for nothing other than their preordained programming.

In reality, the "more speech" solution of the marketplace model has had a boomarang effect. By flooding individuals with inane, ugly, and indecent speech, it has dulled their senses and diminished their ability to discern quality, much less truth.[52] The "more speech" solution has also adversely affected the nation's democratic process. A deluge of entertainment has had a crowding-out effect on political speech. One study of network television news, for instance, revealed that in 1988 there was an average of 38 minutes per month of coverage of entertainment stories. But just two years later, that average had almost doubled, to 68 minutes.[53]

Audience time is limited, and all speech competes against each other for public attention.[54] Consequently, the greater the supply of easy, hypnotic entertainment, the lower the demand for the more rigorous and thoughtful political speech. In a way, the age of abun-

dant media speech has produced a First Amendment scarcity problem—a scarcity of public attention to the speech of political and
social issues on which a democracy must depend.

With the passage of time, the faults and shortcomings of the marketplace model have become apparent. If competition in the communications marketplace truly did correct all pernicious ideas, then
there would not still be all the violent, racist, hate-filled, and sexually exploitive speech that continues to thrive. Perhaps the reason
why the "good" has not driven out the "bad" is because human
beings do not always base their choices and proclivities on a process of rational thought. Emotion and base instinct play a crucial
role. And it is to emotion and instinct that so much of the electronic
media caters. But this primal appeal to emotion and instinct effectively renders contemporary entertainment programming immune
from competition with rational ideas. The two are as different as
apples and sledgehammers.

Recognizing the primal characteristic of some forms of speech
has led judges to carve out certain exceptions, like obscenity and
fighting words. Because these forms of speech have no truth value,
courts have denied them First Amendment protection. Such "low
value" speech includes lewd or profane speech, which has "no essential part of any exposition of ideas,"[55] and "epithets or personal
abuse," which are "not in any proper sense communication of information or opinion safeguarded by the Constitution."[56] But the judicial creation of "low value" categories is the exception rather than
the rule. Generally, the Court has taken the Holmesian view that
censorship results in a great deal of legitimate speech being lost to
the marketplace, all for no particular social gain.[57] The presumption
is that there is never a good reason to oppose speech or to confine it
to specific listeners. Stifled speech, even if not censored, attains an
almost martyred glory. The presumption is that only the absence of
speech can hurt.

But reality is proving these presumptions wrong. In times of flood,
people learn that water is not always the giver of life. Universities
are learning this lesson. In the 1990s, they experimented with speech
codes in an attempt to do away with perceived racist and sexist attitudes. Now, their aims are less lofty. Now, universities are just trying
to censor all the profanities shouted by the crowds at collegiate athletic events; they are just trying to control the worst elements of
speech so that the events retain some semblance of civility; their

free speech sights are not strictly on the willing speaker, of which there is no shortage, but on the unwilling listener, of which there is likewise becoming no shortage.

The pressing speech issue today, during this age of media proliferation, is not government censorship of dissident political speech. The pressing issue is not one of trying to open the closed gateways to speech. Rather, the issue is one of throwing the listener and viewer a lifeline before she is swept away by the flood.

The First Amendment is not just about increasing the volume and plentitude of speech. It goes much deeper than that, to the roots of human liberty. The First Amendment speech clause is about individual control. It is about the control of one's communicative process. For the speaker, this means the freedom to state her opinions without government punishment. It means the freedom to put those opinions into some avenue of public circulation. This right of control the courts have steadfastly protected; but they have not gone full circle. They have not, aside from isolated situations, given any meaningful control to the listener. They have not recognized any effective legal right to be selective in the speech to which the listener is exposed, certainly not to the degree that the courts have given rights to speakers to expose others to their opinions. In this regard, the courts have failed to recognize the wider communicative aspect of speech; they have only focused on its delivery.

Any viable communicative interchange, which after all is the whole point of protecting speech, involves an exchange of ideas between a willing speaker and a willing listener. But in the great majority of cases, whenever these two are in conflict, whenever a willing speaker confronts an unwilling listener, the courts yield to the rights of the former, ignoring those of the latter. However, in a time of such pervasive media, when the individual is losing the power to be selective about the media diet that she and her children end up consuming, the notion of a First Amendment right of listener control seems warranted by the doctrine of changed circumstances.

Campaign finance regulation essentially tries to enhance the political voice of people who might lack the resources to be heard; or, put another way, such regulations attempt to penalize and repress those groups who are perceived to dominate the political dialogue. In either light, the analogy can be extended to the free speech clause and to reading into the First Amendment a right of control of listeners struggling amidst the domineering influence of the media and its relentless production of entertainment.

There is much hope, a lot of it naive, that technology will provide listeners with greater powers of selectivity. But technology alone cannot give the right of control that inherently resides in the Constitution. Technology alone cannot counteract a First Amendment jurisprudence geared almost exclusively to increasing the quantity of speech and to granting all the communicative rights to speakers.

Notes

1.   *Schenck v. United States*, 249 U.S. 47 (1919).
2.   *Dennis v. United States*, 341 U.S. 494 (1951).
3.   *Yates v. United States*, 354 U.S. 298 (1957).
4.   *Aptheker v. Secretary of State*, 378 U.S. 500 (1964).
5.   *Noto v. United States*, 367 U.S. 290 (1961).
6.   *United States v. Robel*, 389 U.S. 258 (1967).
7.   *Brandenburg v. Ohio*, 395 U.S. 444 (1969); *Hess v. Indiana*, 414 U.S. 105 (1973).
8.   *Cohen v. California*, 403 U.S. 15 (1971).
9.   *Barnes v. Glen Theatre, Inc.*, 501 U.S. 560 (1991).
10. *Hustler Magazine v. Falwell*, 485 U.S. 46 (1988).
11. *Ashcroft v. American Civil Liberties Union*, 535 U.S. 564 (2002).
12. Cass R. Sunstein, "Free Speech Now," 59 *University of Chicago Law Review* 255, 258 (1992).
13. Mark Wigfield, "FCC Reports Spike in Complaints about Broadcast Indecency," *Dow Jones Newswires*, November 21, 2003.
14. James Poniewozik, "The Decency Police," *TIME*, March 28, 2005, 31.
15. Diana West, "All That Trash," *Public Interest*, Summer 2004, 131.
16. Poniewozik, "The Decency Police," 30.
17. "Television Quotes," http://en.thinkexist.com/quotations/television/4.html.
18. Julie Salamon, "The New Faces of Reality TV," *New York Times*, September 26, 2004, AR1.
19. Poniewozik, "The Decency Police," 28.
20. Julie Salamon, "Trading Buggies and Bonnets for Stardom," *New York Times*, July 28, 2004, D1.
21. Stephen L. Carter, *Civility: Manners, Morals, and the Etiquette of Democracy* (New York: Basic Books, 1998), 6.
22. Jacques Steinberg, "FCC to Fine Clear Channel $495,000 Over Stern," *New York Times*, April 9, 2004, C3.
23. Sarah McBride, "Clear Channel Dumps Stern After Big Fine," *Wall Street Journal*, April 9, 2004, B1. As a *New York Times* columnist described the FCC crackdown on indecency, "This is McCarthyism, 'moral values' style." Frank Rich, "Bono's New Casualty: 'Private Ryan,'" *New York Times*, November 21, 2004, AR1.
24. Steven Zak, "Censorship Whining," *Washington Times*, August 2, 2004.
25. William P. Marshall, "In Defense of the Search for Truth as a First Amendment Justification," 30 *Georgia Law Review* 1 (1995).
26. R. Randall Rainey, "The Public's Interest in Public Affairs Discourse, Democratic Governance, and Fairness in Broadcasting," 82 *Georgetown Law Journal* 269, 325 (1993).
27. James Weinstein, "Speech Categorization and the Limits of First Amendment Formalism," 54 *Case Western Reserve Law Review* 1091, 1101 (2004).
28. Carter, *Civility*, 171.

29. Alexander Meiklejohn, *Free Speech and Its Relation to Self-Government* (New York: Harper, 1948); Robert C. Post, *Constitutional Domains: Democracy, Community, Management* (Cambridge, Ma.: Harvard University Press, 1995).

30. Lillian R. BeVier, "The First Amendment and Political Speech," 30 *Stanford Law Review* 299 (1978).

31. Sunstein, "Free Speech Now," 293.

32. William Galston, "Liberal Virtues and the Formation of Civic Character," in *Seedbeds of Virtue*, Mary Ann Glendon and David Blankenhorn, eds. (New York: Madison Books, 1995), 57.

33. Carter, *Civility*, 158.

34. Children's Defense Act of 1999, H.R. 2036, 106th Cong. (1999) §5(a)(4).

35. Abby Schloessman Risner, "Violence, Minors and the First Amendment," 24 *St. Louis University Public Law Review* 243, 268 (2005).

36. *Grosjean v. American Press Co.*, 297 U.S. 233, 245-250 (1936).

37. *Arkansas Writers' Project, Inc. v. Ragland*, 481 U.S. 221, 231 (1987).

38. Brian K. Pinaire, "A Funny Thing Happened on the Way to the Market," 27 *Journal of Law & Politics* 489, 503 (2001).

39. See *Sable Communications of California, Inc. v. F.C.C.*, 492 U.S. 115 (1989); *United States v. Playboy Entertainment Group, Inc.*, 529 U.S. 803 (2000); *Reno v. American Civil Liberties Union*, 521 U.S. 844 (1997).

40. See *Frisby v. Schultz*, 487 U.S. 474, 481 (1988); *Board of Education v. Pico*, 457 U.S. 853, 866 (1982); *Citizens Against Rent Control v. City of Berkeley*, 454 U.S. 290, 295 (1981); *Bigelow v. Virginia*, 421 U.S. 809, 826 (1975); *Time, Inc. v. Hill*, 385 U.S. 374, 382 (1966).

41. Ashutosh Bhagwat, "Of Markets and Media: The First Amendment, the New Mass Media, and the Political Components of Culture," 74 *North Carolina Law Review* 141, 161 (1995).

42. *Erznoznik v. City of Jacksonville*, 422 U.S. 205, 210 (1975).

43. *Abrams v. United States*, 250 U.S. 616 (1919).

44. John Milton, "A Speech for the Liberty of Unlicensed Printing, To the Parliament of England," in *Prose Writings* 23-28 (1927); J. S. Mill, *On Liberty*, Gertrude Himmelfarb, ed. (Penguin, 1974 [1859]), 75-118.

45. Patrick M. Garry, "Oliver Wendell Holmes and the First Amendment," in *Great Justices of the U.S. Supreme Court*, William Pederson and Norman Provizer, eds. (New York: Peter Lang Publishers, 1993), 135.

46. Ibid., 139.

47. *Abrams v. United States*, 250 U.S. 616, 629 (1919).

48. Ronald Adelman, "The First Amendment and the Metaphor of Free Trade," 38 *Arizona Law Review* 1125, 1166 (1996).

49. Christopher Yoo, "The Rise and Demise of the Technology-Specific Approach to the First Amendment," 91 *Georgetown Law Review* 245, 279 (2003).

50. R. Randall Rainey, "The Public's Interest in Public Affairs Discourse, Democratic Governance, and Fairness in Broadcasting," 82 *Georgetown Law Journal* 269, 297 (1993).

51. *Madsen v. Women's Health Center*, 512 U.S. 753, 774 (1994).

52. "Discretion, a fragile virtue at best, is almost impossible to cultivate in a wholly uncensored culture like our own." West, "All That Trash," 131.

53. J. Max Robins, "Nets' Newscasts Increase Coverage of Entertainment, *Variety* 3, 63 (July 18, 1990).

54. J. M. Balkin, "Some Realism about Pluralism: Legal Realist Approaches to the First Amendment," 1990 *Duke Law Journal* 375, 409 (1990).

55. *Chaplinsky v. New Hampshire*, 315 U.S. 568, 572 (1942).

56.   *Cantwell v. Connecticut*, 310 U.S. 296, 309 (1940).
57.   Steven Gey, "The Case Against Postmodern Censorship Theory," 145 *University of Pennsylvania Law Review* 193, 221 (1996).

2

The First Amendment Right of Control

Personal Autonomy and Communicative Control

The First Amendment speech clause is not just about speaking. More fundamentally, it is about individual control—the ability to control one's communicative activities.[1] The speech clause is not about making sure that every bit of speech can flow unimpeded to every member of the public (as the marketplace metaphor envisions); it is about each person being able to decide what ideas are right for consideration.[2] Yet, the more that media speech becomes ubiquitous, the more power people need to control it. Like water, speech is a vital thing, but not when it floods. So far, though, First Amendment doctrines have barely recognized this flood and the suffocating effects it can have. They have not considered the plight of the individual in a 500-channel world.

Underlying any individual freedom or right is the ability to control. As Steven Heyman argues, liberty of speech should be understood "as part of the right to control one's own person."[3] It is the individual's right to control that confers freedom. This is the fundamental test of liberty. Control defines individual autonomy, and individual autonomy is at the very root of the freedoms laid out in the Bill of Rights.

As has been so often stated by both courts and scholars, the free speech clause of the First Amendment serves to guarantee individual autonomy in matters of speech and personal beliefs. According to C. Edwin Baker, the key principle underlying the First Amendment is the "respect for individual integrity and autonomy...to use speech to develop herself or to influence or interact with others in a manner that corresponds to her values."[4] In the past, this notion of autonomy has been applied primarily to speakers, protecting them in their freedom to define and develop themselves through their individual speech.[5] But autonomy can also be applied to listeners, especially since most people in the public domain spend more time taking in the speech of others than in putting out their own speech. Consequently, for many, personal growth and self-realization will be determined more by the ideas and images they receive from other speakers than by those they express themselves.

Speech is a component of something larger: the communicative process. Outside this process, speech is a useless and irrelevant endeavor. Moreover, speech is not just an individual act; it is a social act as well. Freedom of speech, then, is the liberty to engage in the social act of communication and to form certain social relationships. So in the course of protecting speech, the First Amendment really protects this social, communicative process. Therefore, to analyze speech, one must look to the broader context of this process. And if speech is to be viewed within this larger communicative process, then the speaker cannot be given exclusive privilege. Nor can the self-realization of the speaker be allowed to dominate over the self-realization of the other participants in the process.[6]

The opposing argument that is incorporated within the marketplace model is that any constitutional concession to listeners could well translate into a de facto system of social censorship that would only stifle individual freedom. While this argument has some merit, it also patronizes listeners, not trusting them to have any real freedom to choose. Yet if a free and open communicative process is to have any meaning, it must be a process involving autonomous participants. For the listener, this means the ability to decide for herself what ideas she will incorporate into forming her own convictions—what images and opinions she will consider in deciding what is good in life, bad in politics, false in faith, and beautiful in art. If autonomy is synonymous with self-determination, and if the First Amendment seeks to insure individual autonomy, then an autonomous individual should have the right to choose what images and ideas from the outside world to reject having one's character exposed to.[7] Just as a person has the right to speak or be silent, so too should a listener have the right to listen or reject. In a case in which an Indiana state court judge rejected a constitutional challenge to Indiana's no-call list, Circuit Court Judge Carl Heldt stated: "Although the First Amendment imposes strict limitations on government actions that interfere with the free exchange of ideas, the First Amendment does not stand as an impediment to private decisions to give audience to certain types of speech while avoiding others."[8]

The kind of communicative process envisioned by the First Amendment requires that all participants—speaker and listener—be free to join or leave that process, to affirm or reject the ideas conveyed during that process, to strengthen or sever at any time the communicative relationship. Just as a speaker should be free to achieve self-fulfillment through expressing his thoughts, a listener should be free from being exposed to speech that violates her sense of autonomy and self-realization. Just as a person should be free from emotional distress at the hands of another, so too should she be free from the unwanted intrusion of speech that violates that which sets herself apart from others—her sense of self dignity and integrity.[9] A truly free communicative process means that both speakers and listeners are equal in their ability to participate. Under such an equality, speakers should not have a greater right to force their speech on unwilling listeners than those unwilling listeners have to reject and avoid that speech. Speakers should not be given the right to dominate the communicative process in such a way that forces unwilling listeners to simply relent.

Some scholars propose a complete shift from a speaker-centered view of free speech to an audience-centered view.[10] This proposal would cast freedom of expression strictly as a right of audiences to receive the speech, not as a right of speakers to speak. But this exclusive focus on audiences has the same fault as the more traditional and singular focus on speakers. Both approaches fail to incorporate the two-sided nature of communication. Indeed, the constitutional guarantee of free speech is undermined by excluding consideration of the interests of either speaker or listener. Instead, what is needed is a more balanced First Amendment approach, one that encompasses both speaker and listener rights. Just as it protects the ability of individuals to speak, the First Amendment should also seek to safeguard an individual's desire to reject unwanted communications. Such a balanced approach, mindful of listener autonomy, is especially needed given the "changed circumstances" caused by the pervasiveness of media speech in modern society.

Judicial Recognition of a Right of Control—The Right to Filter

Although the courts have never recognized a specific right of listener control, they have acknowledged and upheld various aspects of that right. As a starting point, the Court has stated that "at the heart of the First Amendment lies the principle that each person should decide for himself or herself the ideas and beliefs deserving of expression, consideration, and adherence."[11] The Court has also stated that the ability to avoid unwanted communications is a vital component of "individual autonomy."[12] Furthermore, a right to avoid listening might well flow from the right to affirmatively listen that is contained in the First Amendment. The Court has acknowledged that "full capacity for individual choice...is the presupposition of First Amendment guarantees."[13] And in two political speech cases—*FEC v. Massachusetts Citizens for Life, Inc.*[14] and *Austin v. Michigan State Chamber of Commerce*[15]—the Court, at least in dicta, suggested that the marketplace of ideas may be regulated so as to temper the domineering voices of a few speakers. This suggestion might well apply to regulations helping individuals exercise their private right to censor by screening out unwanted, pervasive entertainment programming.

To control information is to filter it. Filtering, or editing, has been going on since human beings first began communicating. The greater the supply of information, the greater the need for editing.[16] Constitutional recognition of a right to edit occurred in *Miami Herald Publishing Co. v. Tornillo.*[17] In *Tornillo*, the Court upheld the right of newspapers to edit their content as they saw fit, without any outside constraints. Later, in *Denver Area Educational Telecommunications Consortium, Inc. v. FCC*, the Court affirmed the right of cable operators to edit sexually explicit programming.[18] In the Communications Decency Act of 1996, Congress even encouraged Internet providers to edit out sexually offensive material by granting them immunity from libel and defamation suits regarding any content decisions made in the course of that self-regulatory function.[19]

Aside from the specific issue of editing, there is also judicial support for a general right to exclude various kinds of speech. Courts have allowed time-manner-place restrictions to completely prohibit certain means of conveying speech, especially when those means serve to cause an "information overload" to people in a specific geographic area. For instance, in *Heffron v. International Society for Krishna Consciousness*, the Court upheld a statute that forbad members of a religious sect from distributing their religious material in face-to-face encounters with State Fair attendees, ruling that the First Amendment "does not guarantee the right to communicate one's views...in any manner that may be desired."[20] Similarly, in *International Society for Krishna Consciousness v. Lee*, a regulation prohibiting Society members from soliciting at airports was upheld.[21]

Previously, in *Cox v. New Hampshire*, the Court had upheld a statute prohibiting anyone from conducting a parade or procession on public streets without a valid license.[22] In *Madsen v. Women's Health Center, Inc.*, the Court even sustained an injunction preventing protestors from entering a 36-foot buffer zone around abortion clinics.[23] And in *Members of the City Council of Los Angeles v. Taxpayers for Vincent*, the Court sustained an ordinance that completely prohibited the posting of signs (even political posters) on public property.[24] According to the Court, "the visual assault on the citizens of Los Angeles presented by an accumulation of signs posted on public property constitutes a significant substantive evil within the city's power to prohibit."[25]

But the strongest and most recent judicial pronouncement on filtering rights occurred in *United States v. American Library Association*, where the Court was presented with a constitutional challenge to the Children's Internet Protection Act ("CIPA"), which required all public libraries receiving federal assistance for Internet access to install filtering software that would block pornographic material from appearing on any computer terminal.[26] Facing the Court was a host of concerns, including the availability and amount of pornographic material on the Internet, the ability of children to access that pornography, the interest of parents in shielding children from Internet pornography, and the difficulties in doing so without some outside assistance. Also facing the Court was the precedent previously set in *Board of Education v. Pico*.[27]

Pico involved a constitutional challenge to a school library's decision to remove certain books from its collection. The removal occurred after the local school board, due to pressure from a group of parents, had directed that a list of books be taken off the library shelves.[28] The board characterized the books as "just plain filthy," asserting that "it is our duty, our moral obligation, to protect the children in our schools from this moral danger as surely as from physical and medical dangers."[29] In its opinion, the Supreme Court focused on the distinction between removing books from the library and acquiring them in the first place.[30] The Court recognized that school boards have broad discretion in the management of school affairs, and that "local school boards must be permitted to establish and apply their curriculum in such a way as to transmit community values."[31] But this discretion, though applicable to the acquisition of library books, did not apply to their removal. The Court stated that the government "may not, consistently with the spirit of the First Amendment, contract the spectrum of available knowledge."[32] A removal of books from a library, according to the Court's reasoning, violated the right to receive information—a right that is "an inherent corollary of the rights of free speech."[33]

The *Pico* ruling rested upon a precise distinction. School boards were completely free to decide which books to add to their library; but once the book was placed on the shelf, all freedom of discretion ended. Once in possession of speech material, school authorities could only expunge that material in certain narrowly defined circumstances. Apparently, according to the Court, the First Amendment only allowed freedom in the acquisition of new speech, never in the subsequent editing or use of that speech. But *Pico* was a decision not yet confronting the flood of speech produced in an Internet world.

Sixteen years later, *Pico* served as a guiding precedent for one of the first Internet filtering cases to be litigated.[34] In *Mainstream Loudoun v. Board of Trustees*, an association of patrons sued the county library for installing on its Internet computers filtering software that blocked out certain pornographic material.[35] The *Loudoun* court relied heavily on *Pico*, agreeing with the plaintiffs that blocking out unwanted Internet sites was similar to removing a library book because of disagreement with its content.[36] By purchasing Internet access, the "library had made all Internet publications instantly accessible to its patrons," and that "by purchasing one such publication, the library had purchased them all," the court found.[37] In likening the Internet to a collection of encyclopedias, the court saw the library's failure to provide access to a select portion of sites as analogous to blacking out disagreeable portions of those encyclopedias. Thus, although the library had not even viewed a minute fraction of the hundreds of millions of sites existing on the worldwide web, by granting Internet access to its patrons it had completely given up any freedom to then filter the information or images available through that access. The *Loudoun* court essentially gave librarians, in connection with the Internet, no other choice than a take-it-or-leave-it. It was like signing up for cable, and then being forced to accept whatever the cable company gave you, even if it included the Playboy Channel.

Both *Pico* and *Loudoun* implicitly recognized a right to edit or exclude. But they qualified that right, giving it power only if done at the point of acquisition of information. As the years progressed and the Internet expanded, however, this qualification began to appear overly simplistic, ignoring the realities of the information age. Given the constantly increasing material being generated over the Internet, it could hardly be reasonable to expect that editing decisions could all be made at some initial, acquisitive point in the process. In *United States v. American Library Association*, the Court addressed this issue.

In the years leading up to the *American Library Ass'n* decision, the use of filtering software in libraries had become the biggest free speech controversy since the Communications Decency Act.[38] In the past, librarians had struggled with monitoring minors' access to various controversial texts, but these struggles were minimal compared to the headaches brought on by the Internet's endless rows of cyber-shelves.[39] With the Internet, libraries faced the continual question of whether to make content-based decisions regarding access to certain online sources.[40] The Court recognized that "there is an enormous amount of pornography on the Internet, much of which is easily obtained," and that the "accessibility of this material has created serious problems for libraries, which have found that patrons of all ages, including minors, regularly search for online pornography."[41] Furthermore, according to the Court, library patrons would "expose others to pornographic images by leaving them displayed on Internet terminals or printed at library printers."[42]

By upholding the filtering requirement, the *American Library Ass'n* Court took a different view of a library's role than did the court in *Loudoun*. It saw the librarian more as an editor and selector than as a provider of unlimited information: The librarian's responsibility "is to separate out the gold from the garbage, not to preserve everything."[43] The Court did not see librarians as serving a recipient's right to view everything existing within the marketplace of information. "Because of the vast quantity of material on the Internet, and the rapid pace at which it changes, libraries cannot possibly segregate, item by item, all the Internet material that is appropriate for inclusion from all that is not," the Court stated.[44] In other words, in a world of the Internet, there has to be a freedom to filter. Moreover, implicit in the Court's decision was the acknowledgment that speakers have a right to speak, but that intermediaries and users have a right to edit.[45] And this freedom to filter can justify certain burdens on the access to sexually explicit speech.

Protecting the Speech of the Inarticulate

For most individuals unable to inject their voice into the stream of mass media programming, censorship is their only way of participating in the marketplace of public communications. In the modern world, censorship may well be the speech of the inarticulate, the media-outsiders. The only way to voice one's opinion about a particular message or image in the social marketplace may be to simply accept or reject it. But even this simple opinion may not be so easy to register or voice. Take, for instance, messages appearing on television. More than eighty-five percent of households subscribe to cable or satellite TV. Therefore, once the cable is hooked up and the installation fee is paid, and the automatic bill payment set up through the consumer's bank, all the messages and images conveyed through all the cable and broadcast channels are already accepted. The real challenge becomes how to reject those images and ideas that are found offensive or revolting. There is no easy way to do that, no automatic system of rejection similar to the automatic bill payment system. Moreover, if individuals are to have the right to privately censor, that right must be more than theoretical.

In 1991, the Pennsylvania state legislature passed a law regulating the size of vulgarities on bumper stickers. It limited the height and width of letters used to spell six specific words describing bodily functions and sex acts. Threatening suit to challenge the constitutionality of this statute, an ACLU spokesperson offered this advice to motorists caught behind a car with a vulgar bumper sticker: Instead of looking at the vulgarity, "you can look at traffic, the trees, the cars around you."[46] This is the "averting your eyes" solution to offensive speech. In reality, though, how can a motorist possibly avert her eyes from the car in front of her? If that is the extent of her ability to censor, then she effectively has no such ability. Likewise, parents cannot realistically chase their children around all day to monitor the television they watch, the music they listen to, and the video games they play. The media is too pervasive for parents to keep up with it. They need some help to perform their parental duties, just as they need safety caps on medicine bottles, and age limits for purchasing cigarettes, and ingredient labels on food items.

By granting to individuals the power to facilitate a private right to censor, the courts can give some autonomy to the unwilling listener wishing to exert some control over his or her communicative environment, dominated by a pervasive media presence. Justice Brandeis once wrote that "the greatest menace to freedom is an inert people" and that "the final end of the State was to make men free to develop their faculties."[47] Given the modern media culture, a private right to censor is needed if for no other reason than to make possible some individual action in society's communications marketplace. A private right to censor may be an individual's only means of expressing her views on the state of public discourse. It may be the only way that the individual can attempt to place some norms of civility or decency on the public communication entering and influencing that individual's life. It may even be the only way in which individuals may retain their democratic voice. As at least one scholar has noted, "explicit sex talk" could well be "disempowering and silencing" to sizable groups in society, including feminists and cultural conservatives.[48]

Not only is a private right to censor necessary for listeners to have some effective individual control within the media culture, but it is also necessary for listeners to revive the position they held in the communications marketplace of the eighteenth century, at the time the First Amendment was adopted, when audiences did not bear the total burden of screening offensive and degrading speech.

The First Amendment and the Preservation of Censorship

With the ratification of the First Amendment, the United States did not banish censorship. Non-governmental censorship continued to thrive, just as it had prior to adoption of the Bill of Rights. Cultural codes strictly regulated the expressive behavior of late-eighteenth century Americans. Religion and social customs discouraged speech that was rude, offensive, degrading, or insulting. Since the great majority of the censorship was culturally-imposed, the law played a relatively minor role.

The influence of social shame also served to regulate public speech.[49] This shame was particularly effective given the small size and isolation of local communities, the intimacy of individuals living in those communities, the fear of being ostracized by the community, and the strict adherence to parental and social authority. As Professor Leonard Levy observes in *Legacy of Suppression*, eighteenth century Americans did not consider freedom of speech to include the expression of obnoxious or detestable ideas.[50]

According to free speech theories prevailing at the time, the First Amendment was not aimed at maximizing the amount of public speech. To the contrary, the types of expression qualifying for protection were limited. Levy argues that the framers of the First Amendment generally adhered to the philosophy of William Blackstone concerning free speech.[51] Under the Blackstonian theory, speech that was defamatory, immoral, subversive, or disturbing of public peace and good order should not be protected.[52] The liberty of speech, like practically every other liberty, was subject to the common good and bounded by the rights of others.[53] Under eighteenth-century notions of natural law, freedom of speech existed only as long as it was not used to injure or control the rights of another.[54] For Blackstone, the function of society was not merely to protect natural rights but to civilize human beings, since morality and public order were the only solid foundations of civil liberty.[55] And on this point—that free speech was limited by the rights of others—even Thomas Jefferson was in agreement.[56]

Eighteenth-century Americans adhered to a kind of "morality of language," recognizing the link between words and social relationships.[57] This morality of language encompassed a belief in civility. It dictated that people should not engage in speech that insults or offends another person. As one eighteenth-century American writer opined, freedom of speech should be confined to the limits set by truthfulness, good taste, and "what is not against Morals or Good Manners."[58] According to Joseph Story, perhaps the foremost nineteenth-century constitutional historian, the claim that the First Amendment "was intended to secure to every citizen an absolute right to speak, or write, or print, whatever he might please, without any responsibility, public or private, therefor, is a supposition too wild to be indulged by any rational man."[59]

Since the settlement of America's first colonies, and persisting until the latter half of the twentieth century, the censorship of morally offensive speech was a consistent occurrence.[60] During the colonial period, authorities regulated speech so as to maintain a moral society.[61] But even after ratifying the Bill of Rights, most states had statutes banning blasphemy and profanity.[62] The first obscenity conviction occurred in the United States in 1815. In *Commonwealth v. Sharpless*, the court ruled that the for-profit showing of a picture of a man and woman in an "indecent posture" constituted a common law offense against public decency.[63] Six years later, Vermont enacted the first law making sexual obscenity a crime.[64] And in 1873, the U.S. Congress passed an anti-obscenity law known as the

Comstock Act. Thus, when profanity and indecency became constitutional rights in the latter part of the twentieth century, they became rights "without any tradition behind [them]," leaving us with "no norms to govern [their] use."[65]

Contrary to current First Amendment doctrines, the focus of free speech theories during the constitutional period was not exclusively on the speaker. As much focus was placed on the harms caused by speech as on the benefits secured by free speech. But over time, the harms caused by unfettered speech became constitutionally demoted, with such harms being characterized as mere social interests.[66] Thus, when First Amendment conflicts now arise between speakers and unwilling listeners, it is the latter who lose out because they can only assert a "social interest" against a constitutional right. Furthermore, contemporary free speech doctrines have generally abandoned the natural rights foundation of the First Amendment, in which free speech was limited by the rights of others.[67] This eighteenth-century natural law principle gave way in the twentieth century to the marketplace model, in which exclusive focus was placed on the speaker and all the possible benefits of speech, rather than on any harms of that speech to listeners.

Because of the nature of public communications in the eighteenth century, listeners did not have to worry about averting their eyes from offensive speech. Not only was such speech effectively constrained by private and cultural censorship practices, but the public communications system was not even remotely as pervasive as today. There were only two forms of media: the newspaper and the public lectern. If someone wished to read a newspaper, they had to go out and find one. It was not delivered to their doorstep. If someone wanted to hear a public lecture or debate, they had to walk to the town hall, early enough to secure a seat. They knew ahead of time the general content of what they were about to read or listen to, and they had to take very deliberate and strenuous efforts to receive that information. Later, as the mass media began to evolve in the late nineteenth century, listeners were still able to avoid an "averting their eyes" problem. For during the Victorian era, it was still considered a taboo to engage in any kind of crude or offensive expression.[68]

Early Americans also seemed to have drawn a distinction between political speech and offensive, non-political speech. Many eighteenth-century state laws specifically prohibited profanity, blasphemy, and lewdness.[69] Moreover, state licensing laws censored entertainment, even though a similar censorship of the press was considered unconstitutional. Laws regulating stage performances and theatrical productions were even passed by the Continental Congress.[70] And throughout the nineteenth century, state regulators continued to monitor the theater.[71] As one scholar has noted, "whatever the First Amendment meant to Madison, Hamilton, Jefferson or Story, it did not have sufficient reach to bar the [censorship] of theatrical presentations."[72]

The Need for Communicative Control

The power and pervasiveness of the modern media makes some level of individual control all the more important. As the Supreme Court has recognized, broadcast and cable programming exert a uniquely pervasive presence in the lives of American children.[73] Through the media, every kind of speech is readily available, sometimes with no more effort than the push of a finger. Consequently, ways are being explored to combat the constant surge of unwanted information and to help the receiver control what he or she receives. Do-not call lists are set up for people who wish to avoid being contacted by telemarketers. Legislators debate laws that would require Internet providers to furnish filtering software. Indeed, many Internet users spend as much time avoiding speech as retrieving it, for nowhere is the abundance of speech in contemporary life more evident than in the flood of information flowing out of the Internet. Approximately one trillion spam emails were sent out in 2003 alone.[74] With the explosive growth of the Internet, "it is clear that society is demanding some method for shielding itself, or at the very least for shielding children."[75]

In a world of 500 digital television channels, twenty-four hour cable, and an Internet on which information-carriage increased tenfold from 1997 to 2000,[76] the problem is not too little speech, but too much—and especially, in terms of the kind of speech needed for an informed self-government, too much of the "low value" speech.[77] The Internet contains a plentiful supply of pornography, violence, vulgarity, and hate speech. This is a particularly worrisome problem, since "ninety percent of children between the ages of five and seventeen now use computers."[78] Almost 70 percent of the current traffic on the Internet is adult-oriented material,[79] and approximately 200 new pornographic Web sites are created each day.[80] Moreover, online pornography cannot be neatly cordoned off from where children can gain access to it.[81] It is not like the adult bookstore, which has a windowless door through which children are not permitted to step. Online pornography is just a mouse-click away from coming into anyone's home. For instance, someone who types in www.whitehouse.com (instead of www.whitehouse.gov) is immediately channeled into a porn site. Studies have shown that most adult-oriented commercial websites do not use age verification measures, and that about a quarter of them employ practices like mouse trapping that keep users from exiting the site.[82] Moreover, approximately three quarters of them displayed adult content on the first page, which was accessible to everyone.

In recent years, with sexually exploitive reality shows becoming ever more prominent on the schedule, public complaints to the FCC about indecent programming have soared.[83] The number of complaints to the FCC rose to more than 1.4 million in 2004.[84] Consequently, over the years there have been a number of attempts to regulate television programming.[85] Efforts have ranged from extending the indecency and profanity rules to cable and satellite television,[86] to channeling the broadcast of certain adult-themed programming to times when children are less likely to be viewing,[87] to blocking indecent programming completely,[88] to creating a "family hour" during which programming unsuitable for children is not shown.[89] These regulatory attempts have resulted in part from the FCC's failure to enforce rules prohibiting indecent programming between the hours of 6 a.m. and 10 p.m. During the 1990s, both the federal government's and television industry's censorship of sexual explicitness "suddenly seemed to disappear;" and empirical evidence showed a significant rise in the sexual content of television programming.[90] Furthermore, despite the numbers of public complaints, the FCC continues to grant the vast majority of renewal applications by radio and television broadcasters.[91]

From 1990 to 2004, the FCC has been remarkably lax in its oversight of programming content.[92] This laxity, however, stands in sharp contrast to FCC Chairman Newton Minow's threat to broadcasters in 1961 of more regulatory enforcement if they did not remedy the "vast wasteland" of television. Not only did Chairman Minow's warning occur when the Commission's oversight activity was near its peak, but a glance back at the television standards promulgated by the FCC in 1960 shows just how poorly the Commission has been in maintaining its once-minimum expectations of television quality.[93] There was a time when the FCC gave precise guidelines to broadcasters about their public interest obligations, requiring them to include in their programming the following program categories: 1) opportunity for local self-expression, 2) programs for children, 3) religious programs, 4) educational programs, 5) public affairs programs, 6) editorializing by licensees, 7) political broadcasts, 8) agricultural programs, 9) news programs.[94] But the FCC no longer requires from licensees, as it once did, a detailed specification of program types and the amount of time devoted to each. The only program information currently required on licensee renewal forms is a summary of programming devoted to the educational needs of children.[95] And as FCC Commissioner Michael Copps has observed, the FCC's enforcement mechanisms—for instance, money fines—have become simply a "cost of doing business" for broadcasters and are "never going to stop the media's slide to the bottom."[96]

The reluctance of the FCC to take enforcement action is illustrated by one listener's relentless crusade against offending broadcasters. In 1999, David Smith began complaining to the Commission about the indecency of a Chicago drive-time radio show, "Mancow's Morning Madhouse."[97] Over the next three years, Mr. Smith filed more than seventy complaints. Each time, the FCC dismissed the complaint, stating that Mr. Smith had not provided sufficient detail. Smith eventually went to the expense of providing the Commission with a transcript of the entire show in which indecent segments were aired. Finally, the FCC took action, sanctioning the radio station for programs featuring a porn star describing sexual techniques and a segment called B___ Radio, in which women described sexual activities to the accompaniment of moaning.

But if the FCC has not been successful in preventing broadcast indecency, neither have the courts been successful in enforcing obscenity laws. Despite the Court's opinion in *Miller v. California*, which expanded the reach of governmental regulation of obscenity to include materials offensive to the moral standards of the local rather than national community, pornography "grew like weeds in a vacant lot."[98] Eventually, obscenity cases stopped coming to the courts, partly because government agencies abandoned any censorship efforts, and partly because local censorship attempts were "easily evaded by national channels of communication such as mail service, telephone and the internet."[99]

Coinciding with the FCC's lax regulatory approach has been a steady decline in the broadcast industry's efforts at self-regulation.[100] After years of agreeing not to air liquor advertisements, for instance, broadcast television has not only begun airing them, but has laced those advertisements with raw sexual appeal, such as two women mud-wrestling in their underwear. Broadcasters are also showing no willingness to self-regulate the advertisement of sexual-aid products, such as impotency drugs, thus forcing parents to discuss with children topics perhaps considered inappropriate.

Television's inability to regulate itself was particularly evident in the 2004 "Monday Night Football" ad controversy. The ad, placed during the "Monday Night Football" opening segment, showed an actress from the television series "Desperate Housewives" standing in a locker room, wearing only a towel and provocatively asking a football player to skip the game for her. After she dropped the towel, he agreed, and then she jumped into his arms. Following a barrage of complaints from viewers, executives at ABC apologized, agreeing that the advertisement was "inappropriate."[101] But the fact that ABC was obviously unaware of the ad's "inappropriateness" prior to the public outrage is by itself reason enough to doubt its judgment on any matter of public decency or propriety. Or as one media critic reported, the reason ABC aired the ad was that any flak from the FCC was "chicken feed next to the priceless promotion and ratings bonanza" the network would get from the controversy.[102]

Finally, with respect to the V-chip, the television industry is proving to be anything but cooperative. Despite demands from parent groups, the industry has refused to adopt a ratings system that would expressly identify the amount of sex, violence, and vulgar language in each program. Children's advocacy groups oppose the current "age-appropriateness" rating system as ineffective, because it does not provide parents with enough content information, such as violence, sexual portrayals, and sexually charged language.[103] Furthermore, a study by the Parents Television Council found that during the "sweeps" periods more than half the network programs surveyed were missing the proper content warnings. Ninety-two percent of shows with sexual behavior carried no "S" rating, and 75 percent of shows with violence had no "V."[104] Television broadcasters also make no effort to advertise or promote use of the V-chip, nor do they encourage manufacturers to include V-chip directions in the operating manuals for televisions that contain the chip.[105] A survey by the

Kaiser Family Foundation found that almost 40 percent of all parents do not even know that television sets are equipped with a V-chip.[106] Consequently, the V-chip is rarely used by parents.[107] Furthermore, the Parents Television Council has concluded that the V-chip has led to an increase in indecency, rather than a decrease. The group claims that the V-chip has given "networks free reign to push the TV envelope as long as they put the right stamp on it."[108]

The failure to self-regulate is not confined to television. Video game makers likewise have a self-imposed ratings system, yet studies have shown that these manufacturers actively market to under-age children ultra-violent games rated for users seventeen years and older.[109] With respect to the music industry, the Federal Trade Commission has found that the industry's rating system fails to provide enough information about the content of music lyrics for parents to make intelligent decisions about the music their children listen to.[110] Moreover, in addition to the recording industry's "basically useless" labeling system, there was found a complete absence of enforcement of these ratings at the retail level.[111]

The movie industry has also had a history of indifference to or disregard of ratings. Even though the majority of filmgoers are children, Hollywood has turned out more than five times as many R-rated films as G, PG, or PG-13 films during the years 2000 to 2004. Whereas 2,146 films have received R ratings, only 137 films have been rated G and 252 rated PG.[112] Furthermore, the movie industry has been steadily growing more lenient in its ratings, allowing "increasingly more extreme content in any given age-based rating category over time."[113] A study by the Harvard School of Public Health found that a decade of "ratings creep" has permitted more violent and sexually explicit content into films.[114] In addition, according to the study, "age-based ratings alone do not provide good information about the depiction of violence, sex, profanity, and other content."[115] And if those increasingly lenient and ineffective ratings aren't enough, theater chains have recently begun selling "R-cards," which allow teenagers to attend R-rated movies without being accompanied by a parent or guardian. Critics denounce these R-cards as yet another "maneuver around the movie rating system."[116]

Despite all these regulatory failures, however, the public still desires some power of control. Over half of America's television viewers, for instance, think the FCC should put stricter controls on programs with sexual and violent content, while 68 percent think the entertainment industry has lost touch with the moral standards of the audience, and 62 percent think Hollywood lowers the public morality.[117] This desire for more control over television programming was illustrated during the congressional hearings on the V-chip legislation. Strong parental support was found for a technology "that would give them greater control to block video programming in the home."[118] Such control is growing increasingly vital, especially since, according to a 2004 study by the Kaiser Family Foundation and the Children's Digital Media Centers, there has been "an explosion in electronic media marketed at the very youngest children in our society." The Kaiser Foundation study confirmed that young people "have become viewing, listening and surfing addicts."[119] The report also states that eight- to eighteen-year-olds "live media-saturated lives," spending over forty-four hours per week with electronic entertainment. The 6.5 hours a day devoted to electronic entertainment compares with 1.5 hours spent in physical exercise and just fifty minutes on homework.

A Harvard University study published in *Pediatrics* likewise concludes that American children watch television more than partaking in any other activity, except sleeping.[120] The average child watches nearly three hours of television a day, in addition to the more than five hours devoted each day to other electronic entertainment.[121] But this is not all under the control of parents. Television is so pervasive that children can watch forbidden shows while over at a friend's house, or while attending a birthday party at a pizza restaurant, or while at a gymnasium or workout facility engaging in some athletic function. Or perhaps their friends record a forbidden program, and then replay it on a DVD player or VCR. In addition are all the times when children have to ride in someone else's car, to be picked up from school or daycare or a ball game or choir practice, and are able to listen to whatever sexually explicit talk show or music lyrics might be playing on that person's car radio. To personally monitor every minute of a child's possible exposure to media is near impossible. Moreover, it is folly to think that, in today's world, a person or family can simply "turn everything off" and proceed untouched by the media and its "pop-culture" messages.

Compound this media pervasiveness with the might of media monopoly, and parental control dwindles even further. The vast majority of cable operators, for instance, occupy monopoly positions in their service area.[122] This monopoly power allows them to package their programming in any way they choose, regardless of consumer desires. If a person wants to watch news on CNN, they must also purchase MTV. If they want to watch programs on the Discovery Channel, they must subscribe to a cable service that brings them "The Howard Stern Show" on the E channel. Television is perhaps the only business in the world in which consumers must purchase products they do not want in order to get the products they do want.

Add all these factors together, and the only conclusion is to give individuals a more effective means of controlling their own media exposure. Given the failures of government oversight and industry self-regulation, the only remaining and constitutionally viable solution is to give individuals a greater power to privately censor.

*   *   *

During the 1950s and 1960s, the anti-television activists may have been a little paranoid and extremist in their attacks. And the liberal crusaders fighting fraud and deception on television game shows during the 1950s, as depicted in the movie *Quiz Show*, now seem almost laughable in their naivety. Imagine holding congressional hearings to investigate whether a "reality" television show was being deceptive in its portrayals of reality; imagine calling to task a television network and its executives for producing programming that manipulated the emotions of viewers and fed them "prepreprogrammed" reality. But fifty years later, protests of television programming certainly cannot be blamed on mere paranoia.

Notes

1. Jerry Berman and Daniel Weitzner, "Abundance and User Control: Renewing the Democratic Heart of the First Amendment in the Age of Interactive Media," 104 *Yale Law Journal* 1619, 1621 (1995) (making the argument that the way to an open, interactive communication system is through "user control"—giving individuals a right of shut off).
2. *Turner Broadcasting System v. F.C.C.*, 512 U.S. 622, 641 (1994).
3. Steven Heyman, "Ideological Conflict and the First Amendment," 78 *Chicago-Kent Law Review* 531, 568 (2003).
4. C. Edwin Baker, *Human Liberty and Freedom of Speech* (New York: Oxford University Press, 1989), 59.
5. Steven Heyman, "Righting the Balance: An Inquiry Into the Foundations and Limits of Freedom of Expression," 78 *Boston University Law Review* 1275, 1326 (1998).
6. Heyman, "Righting the Balance," 1348.
7. *Harris v. Forklift Systems*, 510 U.S. 17, 21 (1993).
8. "No-Call Plaintiff Mulls Options," *Evansville Courier & Press*, July 9, 2002, B1.

9.   Heyman, "Righting the Balance," 1332.
10. Scanlon, "A Theory of Freedom of Expression," in *The Philosophy of Law*, R. M. Dworkin, ed. (London; New York: Oxford University Press, 1977), 153.
11. *Turner*, 512 U.S. 622, 641(1994).
12. *Rowan v. United States Post Office*, 397 U.S. 728, 736 (1970).
13. *Bellotti v. Baird*, 443 U.S. 622, 635 (1979).
14. *Federal Election Commission v. Massachusetts Citizens for Life, Inc.*, 479 U.S. 238 (1986).
15. *Austin v. Michigan Chamber of Commerce*, 494 U.S. 652 (1990).
16. Justin Long, "Plugged In," *Reno Gazette-Journal*, June 16, 2003, E3 ("[W]e are all drowning in information"); David Adams, "Spinning Around," *Sydney Morning Herald*, May 20, 2003, 7 ("The Challenge is not so much to get hold of [information] as it is to be discriminate about what we do expose ourselves to").
17. *Miami Herald Pub. Co. v. Tornillio*, 418 U.S. 241, 258 (1974) (ruling that editing is a constitutionally protected function); *Hurley v. Irish-American Gay, Lesbian and Bisexual Group*, 515 U.S. 557, 573 (1995) (holding that the First Amendment protects the freedom to create one's own mix of speech).
18. *Denver Area Education Telecommunications Consortium, Inc. v. F.C.C.*, 518 U.S. 727 (1996).
19. *Zeran v. America Online, Inc*, 129 F.3d 327, 331 (1997).
20. *Heffron v. International Society for Krishna Consciousness, Inc.*, 452 U.S. 640, 647 (1981).
21. 505 U.S. 672 (1992).
22. 312 U.S. 569 (1941).
23. 512 U.S. 753 (1994).
24. *Members of the City Council of City of Los Angeles v. Taxpayers for Vincent*, 466 U.S. 789 (1984).
25. Ibid., 807.
26. *United States v. American Library Association*, 539 U.S. 194, (2003).
27. *Board of Education, Island Trees Union Free School District v. Pico*, 457 U.S. 853 (1982).
28. Ibid., 856-8.
29. Ibid., 857.
30. Ibid., 862.
31. Ibid., 864.
32. Ibid., 866.
33. Ibid., 867.
34. R. Polk Wagner, "Filters and the First Amendment," 83 *Minnesota Law Review* 755, 773 (1999).
35. *Mainstream Loudoun v. Board of Trustees of Loudoun County Library*, 2 F.Supp.2d 783, 787 (1998).
36. Ibid., 793.
37. Ibid.
38. Julia M. Tedjeske, "Mainstream Loudoun and Access to Internet Resources in Public Libraries," 60 *University of Pittsburgh Law Review* 1265, 1266 (1999).
39. Eric L. Wee, "Library Chief Seeks Full Web Access: Proposal Calls for Filters on Computers for Children," *Washington Post*, July 5, 1997, V1.
40. Ibid., 1267.
41. *American Library Association*, 539 U.S. 194, 200 (2003).
42. Ibid.
43. Ibid., 204.

44. Ibid., 195.
45. Tedjeske, "Mainstream Loudoun and Access to Internet Resources in Public Librar-ies," 1291 (discussing a librarian's right of "content-based selectivity or editorial control").
46. William A. Donohue, *Twilight of Liberty: the Legacy of the ACLU* (New Brunswick, New Jersey: Transaction Publishers, 1990), 190.
47. *Whitney v. California*, 274 U.S. 357, 375 (1927).
48. Lili Levi, "The Hard Case of Broadcast Indecency," 20 *Review of Law & Social Change* 49, 156-57 (1993).
49. Phaedra Athena O'Hara Kelly, "The Ideology of Shame," 77 *North Carolina Law Review* 783, 805 (1999).
50. Leonard W. Levy, *Legacy of Suppression: Freedom of Speech and Press in Early American History* (Cambridge: Harvard University Press, 1960).
51. Ibid., 3.
52. William Blackstone, *Commentaries on the Laws of England*, St. George Tucker ed. (William Young Birch, and Abraham Small; Robert Carr, Printer, 1969 [1803]), 151-54.
53. Ibid., 125; Heyman, "Ideological Conflict and the First Amendment," 569.
54. John Trenchard and Thomas Gordon, "Cato's Letters No. 15," in *Cato's Letters, or, Essays on Liberty, Civil and Religious, and other important subjects*, vol. 1, Ronald Hamowy ed. (Indianapolis, Ind: Liberty Fund 1995 [1755]), 110.
55. Heyman, "Righting the Balance,"1285, 1287.
56. Ibid., 1291
57. Debora Shuger, "Civility and Censorship in Early Modern England," in *Censor-ship and Silencing*, Robert C. Post ed. (Los Angeles: The Getty Research Institute Publications and Exhibitions Program, 1995), 98.
58. Levy, *Legacy of Suppression*, 115.
59. Joseph Story, *Commentaries on the Constitution of the United States*, Vol. 3, §1874 (DaCapo Press, 1970 [1891]), 731.
60. H. Franklin Robbins, Jr. and Steven G. Mason, "The Law of Obscenity—Or Ab-surdity?" 15 *St. Thomas Law Review* 517, 520 (2003).
61. Larry Eldridge, *A Distant Heritage: The Growth of Free Speech in Early America* (New York: New York University Press, 1994), 9.
62. Ibid., 540.
63. 2 Serg. & Rawle 91 (Sup. Ct. Penn., 1815).
64. 1821 Vt. Acts & Resolves XXXII, No. 1, §23.
65. Stephen L. Carter, *Civility: Manners, Morals, and the Etiquette of Democracy* (New York: Basic Books, 1998), 69.
66. Steven Heyman, "Righting the Balance," 1306.
67. Ibid., 1299.
68. Carter, *Civility*, 138.
69. Eldridge, *A Distant Heritage*, 6.
70. Jon M. Garon, "Entertainment Law," 76 *Tulane Law Review* 559, 633 (2002).
71. Ibid., 634.
72. Ibid.., 635.
73. *Denver Area*, 518 U.S. 727, 744-45 (1996).
74. Erika Hallace Kikuchi, "Spam in a Box," 10 *Boston University Journal of Science and Technology Law* 263, 266 (2004).
75. Thomas Nachbar, "Paradox and Structure: Relying on Government Regulation to Preserve the Internet's Unregulated Character," 85 *Minnesota Law Review* 215, 218 (2000).

76. Madeleine Schachter, *Law of Internet Speech*, 2nd ed. (Durham, N.C.: Carolina Academic Press, 2002), 16.
77. Volokh, *The First Amendment: Problems*, 114-7.
78. Mitchell P. Goldstein, "Congress and the Courts Battle Over the First Amendment: Can the Law Really Protect Children From Pornography on the Internet?" 21 *John Marshall Journal of Computer and Information Law* 141,143 (2003).
79. Elizabeth M. Shea, "The Children's Internet Protection Act of 1999: Is Internet Filtering Software the Answer?" 24 *Seton Hall Legislative Journal* 167, 174 (1999).
80. H.R. REP. No. 105-775, 10 (1998).
81. Goldstein, "Congress and the Courts," 21 *Journal of Computer & Information Law* 141,144 (2003).
82. Ibid., 144-45.
83. "FCC Chief: TV Gets Too Racy," *The Cincinnati Post*, November 22, 2002, A2.
84. Stephen Labaton, "Knowing Indecency Wherever He Sees It," *New York Times*, March 28, 2005, C1.
85. David L. Bazelon, "FCC Regulation of the Telecommunications Press," 1975 *Duke Law Journal* 213, 228 (1975).
86. Stephen Labaton, "Knowing Indecency Wherever He Sees It," *New York Times*, March 28, 2005, C1.
87. *F.C.C. v. Pacifica Found.*, 438 U.S. 726 (1978).
88. *Denver Area*, 518 U.S. 727 (1996).
89. *Writers Guild of Am., West, inc. v. F.C.C.*, 423 F. Supp. 1064 (C.D. Cal. 1976).
90. Richard A. Brisbin, "Sex on the Tube," *Focus on Law Studies* (ABA) Fall 2004, 6. Empirical evidence showed a significant rise in the use of sexual content on television. Ibid.
91. Christopher Yoo, "The Rise and Demise of the Technology-Specific Approach to the First Amendment," 91 *Georgetown Law Review* 245, 258 (2003).
92. Ronald W. Adelman, "The First Amendment and the Metaphor of Free Trade," 38 *Arizona Law Review* 1125, 1163 (1996); Richard E. Wiley and Lawrence W. Secrest, "Recent Developments in Program Content Regulation," 57 *Federal Communications Law Journal* 235, 235 (2005).
93. Newton N. Minow, "Address to the National Association of Broadcasters" (May 9, 1961), reprinted in Newton N. Minow and Craig L. LeMay, *Abandoned in the Wasteland: Children, Television, and the First Amendment* (New York: Hill and Wang, 1995), 185-96.
94. *En Banc Programming Statement*, 44 F.C.C. 2303 (1960).
95. Children's programming continues to be regulated pursuant to Congress's mandate in the Children's Television Act of 1990, Pub. L. No. 101-437, 104 Stat. 996.
96. Joel Timmer, "The Seven Dirty Words You Can Say on Cable and DBS," 10 *Communication Law and Policy* 179, 181 (2005).
97. Sarah McBride, "One Man's Campaign to Rid Radio of Smut is Finally Paying Off," *Wall Street Journal*, May 13, 2004, A1.
98. William N. Eskridge, Jr., "Some Effects of Identity-Based Social Movements on Constitutional Law in the Twentieth Century," 100 *Michigan Law Review* 2062, 2346 (2002).
99. Ibid.
100. A discussion of the criticisms of media self-regulation is found in Angela J. Campbell, "Self-Regulation and the Media," 51 *Federal Communications Law Journal* 711, 717-19 (1999).
101. Andrea Adelson, "ABC Apologizes for Steamy Intro Monday Night," *Argus Leader*, November 17, 2004, 1C.

102. Jonathan Alter, "A Shabby Fiesta of Hypocrisy," *Newsweek*, November 29, 2004, 56.
103. Lawrie Mifflin, "TV Executives Introduce Rating System," *New York Times*, December 20, 1996, A1.
104. L. Brent Bozell, "The V-Chip is no Magic Pill," *Washington Times*, April 20, 2005.
105. Cass Sunstein, "Philippic.com Republic.Com," 90 *California Law Review* 611, 666 (2002)
106. L. Brent Bozell, "The V-Chip is no Magic Pill." Only 15 percent of parents say they have used the V-chip.
107. Theresa Chidester, "What the #$ is Happening on Television?" 13 *CommLaw Conspectus* 135, 160 (2004).
108. Lynn Elber, "TV Too Nasty for Kids, Study Says," *LA Times*, August 3, 2001, R10.
109. Rupal Ruparel Dalal, "Congress Shall Make No Law Abridging Freedom of Speech—Even If It Causes Our Children to Kill?" 25 *Seton Hall Legislative Journal* 357, 367 (2001).
110. FTC, "Marketing Violent Entertainment to Children: A Review of Self-Regulation and Industry Practices in the Motion Picture, Music Recording & Electronic Game Industries," 27 (September 2000).
111. Senate Commerce, Science, and Transportation Committee, "Marketing Violent Entertainment to Children: A Review of Self-Regulation and Industry Practices in the Motion Picture, Music Recording & Electronic Game Industries," *Federal News Service*, Sept. 13, 2000, 3.
112. Philip F. Anshutz, "Whatever Happened to the Family Film?" *Imprimis*, June 2004, 1.
113. Sharon Waxman, "Study Finds Film Ratings Are Growing More Lenient," *New York Times*, July 14, 2004, B1.
114. Julie Salamon, "The Rating Says PG, But Is That Guidance Enough?" *New York Times*, January 7, 2005, B1.
115. Waxman, "Study Finds Film Ratings Are Growing More Lenient."
116. Micheline Maynard, "Youth Who Like Films Rated R, But Not Chaperones, Get a Card," *New York Times*, June 26, 2004, A15.
117. L. Brent Bozell, "Clean-Up Call," *Washington Times*, April 2, 2005.
118. Howard M. Wasserman, "Second-Best Solution: The First Amendment, Broadcast Indecency, and the V-Chip," 91 *Northwestern University Law Review*, 1223 (1997).
119. Robert Dodge, "Study: Kids Addicted to Media," *Argus Leader*, March 10, 2005, 4A.
120. Renee Boynton-Jarrett et al., "Impact of Television Viewing Patterns on Fruit and Vegetable Consumption Among Adolescents," 112 *Pediatrics* 1321 (December, 2003).
121. Diana West, "All That Trash," *Public Interest*, Summer 2004, 131.
122. Ashutosh Bhagwat, "Of Markets and Media: The First Amendment, the New Mass Media, and the Political Components of Culture," 74 *North Carolina Law Review* 141, 145 (1995).

3

The Constitutional Parameters of a Private Right to Censor

The Need for Such a Right

There has always been a common sense foundation for a private right to censor. Obviously, people do not indiscriminately read or view every bit of speech with which they come in contact. They choose not to read certain books; they refuse to see certain movies; they deliberately refrain from turning on certain television programs. The Constitution would obviously disallow any law that required people to read or view or listen to certain speech, and the courts have frequently reaffirmed the principle that people should be free to choose what they read or view.[1] However, the courts have never constitutionally recognized, except in some narrow and isolated circumstances, any private right to censor. Only in a certain few cases have the courts allowed a burden on speech to be justified by anything remotely resembling a private right to censor;[2] and even then, the decisions have hinged more on privacy concerns that on any individual right to censor.[3] Consequently, the right or ability of a person to censor unwanted speech has been left more or less in a legal limbo. As far as keeping out what speech they don't want, every person is on his own—it is survival of the fittest. Yet to most people, censorship is really the flipside of speech.[4] Living in a world in which public discourse runs primarily through the mass media, individual censorship may be the only way for the common person to participate in that discourse.

Although courts have upheld censorship rights, they have generally done so only when such censorship is being exercised by speakers. In *Denver Area Educational Telecommunications Consortium, Inc. v. FCC*, for instance, the Court sustained a law permitting cable operators to prohibit programming they considered patently offensive.[5] Even the government has legal rights of censorship, if that censorship is done in the course of subsidizing selected speech activities by private actors. In *National Endowment for the Arts v. Finley*, the Court allowed Congress to prohibit the NEA from awarding grants to any project that failed to meet a decency standard.[6] And in *Advocates for the Arts v. Thomson*, the First Circuit upheld a governor's veto of a proposed subsidy for a particular literary magazine that had published an offensive poem.[7] The court noted that decisions on quality were inherent in artistic subsidies and were necessarily subjective.

Just as no democratic society can exist without free speech, no civil society can exist without some form of social censorship to discourage the more destructive and dehumanizing forms of speech. Over the past several decades, however, only negative connotations have been attached to the notion of censorship, as when accusations of censorship are made after a newspaper refuses to print a controversial advertisement, or after a television network agrees not to air a one-sided news story, or even when vulgar graffiti is washed off a public space. Censorship is rarely seen as an attempt for a more civilized life, only as an act of social repression.

Censorship has become one of those words that immediately inspire condemnation, like "Inquisition" and "bigotry" and "witch-hunt" and "intolerance." There is no question that much state censorship of the past was harmful, and that some worthwhile speech was repressed. But likewise, now that there is overabundant, uninhibited speech, there is no question that society is burdened with daunting levels of worthless and harmful speech. Undoubtedly, some speech is better off silenced, particularly when such silencing can be done through social interactions, rather than by direct government regulation. If anything, certain types of social and cultural censorship should be encouraged, not belittled. Verbal abuse and insults serve no worthy goal, and sexually degrading and graphically violent speech have little if any justification. With these forms of speech, social censorship rather than unfettered expression would be the ideal. Silencing, as noted by Professor Schauer, would be the preferred alternative.[8]

In terms of personal autonomy, a private right to censor is on par with the right to speak. Because of the "changed circumstances" of media pervasiveness, however, a private right to censor may now need not only constitutional recognition but governmental support, so as to make it a viable and workable right. Under a private-right-to-censor theory, governmental regulations would not be judged simply by their effects on speakers, but on whether they facilitate a private right to censor within the bounds set for that right. In essence, a private right to censor would elevate listener's rights in the communicative process to a more balanced position with respect to speaker's rights. A private right to censor would confer on individuals a greater ability to give selected elements of the mass media a "no" vote. It would help bring back to the communications marketplace all those people who, because of their opposition to certain messages of the mass media and their inability to counteract those messages, have felt relegated to the margins of society. It would give to all those dwarfed by the mass media a degree of individual control that is presupposed in a democracy.

Whereas the marketplace model focuses exclusively on the speaker's liberty, a private right to censor would expand this focus to include notions of listener equality and social civility. In the past, these notions have always been seen as mere social interests; thus, when the "right" to free speech is set against a mere social "interest," the outcome is more or less predetermined. But a private right to censor would raise these interests to the status of rights, thereby putting them into a more balanced position with respect to speaker freedoms. Consequently, if individuals choose to reject pornographic speech, they do so as a matter of right. Under the existing free speech framework, however, governmental regulations restricting pornography are seen to be simply efforts to protect the social interest in morality, and this justification has never been able to compete with a rights-based approach that looks solely to the speaker's liberty.[9] On the other hand, the First Amendment does not bar regulations against misleading advertising, or laws prohibiting copyright infringement, or convictions for communicative conduct that violates the antitrust laws.[10] Consequently, within the scheme of the First Amendment, listener's rights are certainly as strong as economic interests.

Under the First Amendment, most governmental burdens on a person's ability to publicly express themselves are strictly scrutinized.[11] But no such scrutiny is given to measures that diminish a person's ability to censor. In fact, just the opposite treatment is given to any measure resembling a private right to censor: The measure itself is strictly scrutinized for any adverse effect on the flow of speech.

The vast majority of conflicts between the right to speak and the right to privately censor unwanted speech are resolved in favor of the former. Hence, whatever legal recognition has been given to private censorship rights are almost totally without force.

Clearly, some measures aimed at effectuating a private right to censor may exert a burdensome effect on speech rights. But then, to be effective, the power to censor has to increase as the power of the speech medium increases. Throughout its history, the First Amendment "has had to take on meanings never intended by the founding fathers as technology [produces] forms of speech never before thought imaginable."[12] Therefore, given the judicially-recognized power and intrusiveness of the media, any measures giving people the ability to screen out unwanted messages probably cannot be completely burden-free to the media corporations.

A Shifting of Burdens

Traditional First Amendment analysis focuses on all the possible burdens that any governmental regulation might place on the access or delivery of speech. With respect to listeners who wish to avoid certain offensive speech, however, the courts require that they bear the full burden of "averting their ears."[13] But the growth of a media society, and the corresponding explosion of media speech, have made the burdens of "averting one's eyes" all the more onerous. Likewise, the demise of social customs that once imposed an unofficial censorship on offensive speech have put even more burdens on "averting one's eyes," to the point where it may be nearly impossible to avoid offensive speech. This lopsidedness of burdens has been a natural result of the marketplace metaphor, which focuses only on increasing the amount of social speech.

Given the experience of the constitutional period, it may be a mistake to think of free speech as effortless speech. Adopting a First Amendment model containing a private right to censor does not mean that indecent speech will be suddenly cut off; it means that certain dams may be built to convert a wild rapids of speech into a more controlled flow. There may be some additional burdens or effort needed to access indecent speech, but it will still be available. What a private right to censor seeks to achieve is an equalizing of the burdens, except in the case of political speech.

The Supreme Court decision in *United States v. American Library Association* illustrates this more balanced placement of burdens.[14]

Although the opponents of the filtering law argued that some patrons might be too embarrassed to ask a librarian to unblock certain sites, the Court ruled that "the Constitution does not guarantee the right to acquire information at a public library without any risk of embarrassment."[15] This decision, in its balanced look at the relative burdens involved, followed the parameters of a private right to censor. In so doing, the Court bucked the trend followed in previous cases, in which just about any burden on an adult's access to indecent speech, no matter what the risk to children, was seen as unconstitutional. In *American Library Association*, the goal of protecting children from unwanted speech overshadowed the small burden on adults who could still receive their pornography with just a request to the librarian. It was a decision that took a step toward a First Amendment model recognizing the private right to censor in a media society.

Under the marketplace model, courts dealing with free speech issues have favored opt-out schemes over opt-in ones. Unwilling listeners must opt-out of the unwanted speech environment. They must either constantly monitor their children on the Internet, or else they must pull the plug; they either have to hope and pray as they surf through the cable channels, or else they must disconnect the television. Courts have essentially assumed that the First Amendment requires opt-out.[16] But under a private right to censor, an opt-in requirement can be imposed on certain kinds of "low value" speech in an effort to balance the burdens. If an adult wishes to view indecent programming, he or she must make some effort to opt into it, to access it with some personal identification number. Under such an opt-in scheme, however, there is no decrease in the amount of speech in the system, just a step required before accessing it.

Even though the Court has taken the position that the First Amendment requires opt-out, it has never examined precisely how feasible it is for unwilling viewers or listeners to opt-out, certainly not in the same way that it has examined all the potential burdens placed on those wishing to opt-in. For instance, as Justice Stevens theorized in his opinion in *Reno*, Internet users who wish to shield themselves or their children from pornographic material can essentially build their own technological walls to screen out such offensive material.[17] But this seemingly painless solution is fraught with hidden costs. How many people have access to effective filtering software? And just how effective is that software? And how easily is it disabled? The courts have never factually explored these questions, and yet they presume that opt-in software—software that would essentially require that those wishing to view adult programming take affirmative steps to obtain such programming—is so much more burdensome than is opt-out software. But is it fair that parents of limited resources be compelled to bear the burden of purchasing filters, just so the producers and patrons of pornography not incur the least inconvenience? Is it fair to make parents bear the sole burden of monitoring their children's every interaction with an all-pervasive media, just so that the unfettered freedom of pornographers not be compromised in any way?

A realization of the quantity and accessibility of indecent speech, as well as the potential effects of such speech on minors, has seemingly made the Court more amenable to opt-in schemes. Whereas in *Denver Area* a requirement that people had to make a specific request from their cable operator to receive indecent programming was considered an unconstitutional burden, in *American Library Ass'n* the requirement that adults approach librarians in person to have the blocking software disabled so that they could access sexually explicit sites was not considered an impermissible imposition. Thus, as long as the burdens do not amount to a complete ban, they may be allowable under an opt-in approach that seems to be gaining strength and to which *American Library Ass'n* gave impetus.

Opt-in schemes have been used by other countries to deal with the problem of unwanted information.[18] In the experience of Australia and a number of European countries, an opt-out system tends to favor direct marketers. Furthermore, an opt-in system is "more easily understood and more easily enforced" than opt-out schemes.[19]

An opt-in scheme is like the school voucher program upheld by the Court in *Zelman v. Simmons-Harris*.[20] It helps facilitate choice, by giving individuals the power to choose an option they may not have otherwise had. Seen in this respect, an opposition to a private right to censor would amount to an opposition to the right to choose. Furthermore, an opt-in scheme represented by a private right to censor reflects a more balanced middle ground than the usual dichotomy characterizing traditional free speech thought. Under that dichotomy, there are two polar-opposite systems of speech regulation. One is a system where "top-down regulation of expression is the exception," and the other is a system in which "top-down regulation is the rule."[21] The former is akin to the marketplace model, in which speech is maximized; the latter involves one in which government or social elites make all the decisions about content. A private right to censor, however, attempts to strike a balance between these two divergent systems.

The Political Speech Immunity

Not all speech will be subject to a private right to censor. Generally, the speech covered by this right must meet a three-part test. First, the speech must be that to which children would likely be exposed. Second, the speech must be of a type from which the government has a legitimate interest in shielding children, such as graphic violence, vulgarity, and sexually explicit programming. And third, the speech cannot be political speech. Such speech, as outlined in the theories of Alexander Meiklejohn and described more fully in chapter 6, would be immune from any regulations seeking to facilitate a private right to censor.[22]

According to Meiklejohn, only political speech (or speech that is essential for self-government) should receive full constitutional protection. Meiklejohn's distinction between political and nonpolitical speech is crucial, because only speech that serves the larger cause of promoting democratic processes should receive the highest constitutional protections. Robert Post expands Meiklejohn's theory by arguing that a prime function of free speech is democratic legitimization. According to Post, laws that prohibit potential speakers from engaging in the debate through which public policy is formed "threaten to alienate citizens from their government."[23]

Meiklejohn's self-governance theory seeks to base First Amendment freedoms on a rationale that transcends individual self-fulfillment. Contrary to the precepts of the marketplace model, individual self-fulfillment provides an inadequate foundation for First Amendment freedoms. It fails to distinguish speech in any lasting, constitutional sense. Individuals may experience self-fulfillment in any number of ways—for instance, participating in an athletic event, traveling to new places, sharing the friendship of another—so in this sense speech is no different than many other kinds of human activities. Moreover, even if the act of communication conferred a special feeling of fulfillment upon persons, there would still be no way of distinguishing the act of speaking from the act of listening.

Although the definition of political speech and its application to a private-right-to-censor theory will be discussed at greater length in

chapter 6, suffice it to say here that since the self-governance rationale provides the basic foundation for the First Amendment, and
since political speech is the only speech that serves the purpose of
self-governance, the government is prevented from placing any restrictions on such speech, even if those restrictions do serve a private right to censor.

One benefit of making this political-nonpolitical speech distinction (and thereby subjecting nonpolitical speech to a private right to
censor) is to achieve a simplification of the current, often ambiguous, multi-layered hierarchy of speech containing various levels of
"low value" speech. As it stands now, obscenity, commercial speech,
and "fighting words" all receive different but lesser degrees of constitutional protection. Even though courts have recognized that not
all speech has the same constitutional importance, the snag in this
recognition is how the hierarchy of speech will be distinguished
without invoking the dictatorial hand of government.[24] With a private right of censorship, however, it is the individual who is given
the power to block out what to him or her is low value speech. Since
commercial speech and obscenity clearly qualify as nonpolitical
speech, they would be subject to a private right to censor, which in
turn could provide a more flexible and responsive regulator than the
maize of exceptions and distinctions currently existing within the
marketplace model.

Cases Exemplifying a Private Right to Censor

In *FCC v. Pacifica Foundation*, a case involving an FCC decision
to require broadcasters to channel indecent programming away from
times of the day when there is a reasonable risk that children may be
in the audience, the Court found that the broadcast medium was an
intrusive and pervasive one.[25] In reaffirming that this medium should
receive the most limited of First Amendment protections, the Court
held that the rights of the public to avoid indecent speech trump
those of the broadcaster to disseminate such speech. The Court dismissed the argument that the offended listener or viewer could simply turn the dial and avoid the unwanted broadcast, reasoning that
because the broadcast audience is constantly tuning in and out, prior
warnings cannot protect the listener or viewer from unexpected program content.[26]

Under the private-right-to-censor theory, the general principles of
Pacifica should remain the law. To this day, *Pacifica*'s recognition

of the power and intrusiveness of television still rings true.[27] Due to their "unique pervasiveness," patently offensive broadcasts "confront the citizen, not only in public, but also in the privacy of the home."[28] In *Turner Broadcasting System v. FCC*, the Court likewise recognized the pervasive nature of cable—a finding that in turn rendered cable more susceptible to regulation.[29] Another factor that justified compromising cable operators' speech interests to further those of viewers was the economic power of cable operators, who face "little competition" and can constitute "a kind of bottleneck that controls the range of viewer choice."[30]

Reflecting the parameters of a private right to censor, the D.C. Circuit Court of Appeals in *Action for Children's Television v. FCC* upheld the "safe harbor" provisions of the Public Telecommunications Act of 1992 permitting indecent broadcasts only between 10 p.m. and 6 a.m.[31] In its ruling, the court gave great credence to FCC findings that real parental control over their children's television watching was impossible.[32] The court also found that those parents who wished to expose their children to indecent programming would "have no difficulty in doing so through the use of subscription and pay-per-view cable channels, delayed-access viewing using VCR equipment, and the rental or purchase of readily available audio and video cassettes."[33] The court then concluded that the time-channeling rule for indecent broadcasts did not "unnecessarily interfere with the ability of adults to watch or listen to such materials both because [adults] are active after midnight and...have so many alternative ways of satisfying their tastes at other times."[34]

In *Dial Information Svcs. v. Thornburgh* and *Information Providers' Coalition v. FCC*, two different courts upheld certain federal restrictions on dial-a-porn services.[35] These restrictions—for example, requiring telephone companies to block all access to dial-a-porn services unless telephone subscribers submit written requests to unblock them—were enacted in response to the Supreme Court decision in *Sable* striking down a complete ban on dial-a-porn services. Thus, an important factor leading the courts in *Dial Information Services* and *Information Providers* to rule as they did was the fact that the restrictions did not amount to a complete ban on the indecent speech, but merely shifted the burdens of accessing such speech.

Perhaps best illustrating a private right to censor are two Supreme Court cases that, if such a right were adopted, would be found to have been wrongly decided: *U.S. v. Playboy Entertainment Group* and *Denver Area Educational Telecommunications Consortium, Inc. v. FCC.*[36] At issue in *Denver Area* were regulations in the Cable Act of 1992 requiring cable operators to place indecent programs on a separate, blocked channel, which would be unblocked only after a subscriber submitted a written request for access. In holding these regulations unconstitutional, the Supreme Court was concerned with inconveniences and burdens to potential viewers of indecent programming, including, for instance, the viewer who might want a single show, as opposed to the entire channel, or the viewer who might want to choose a channel without any advance planning (the "surfer"), or the one who worries about the danger to his reputation that might result if he makes a written request to subscribe to the channel. However, none of these burdens presented insurmountable obstacles. Each one of these types of viewers could get access to the desired programming by simply following the established procedures. Furthermore, even though the Court recognized that the purpose of the regulations was to protect minors, that it was a compelling purpose, and that the regulations only applied to sexual material (and not the kind of vitally important political information present, for instance, in the *Pentagon Papers* case[37]), the Court still struck them down. In doing so, the Court affirmed the principle of *Butler v. Michigan,*[38] in that the Constitution does not permit the state to reduce the material available to adults to that which is appropriate only for children. The Court followed this principle even though, in terms of relative burdens, it may be easier for adults to access indecent material than it is for parents to have their children avoid it. Even though the Court acknowledged the invasive nature of television, it refused to let this feature justify the regulations, which still did not amount to a complete ban on the subject speech. Obviously, the Court was singularly focused on the inconveniences to would-be viewers of indecent programming.

The *Denver Area* Court could not arrive at a majority opinion defining the standard of review for regulations of indecent cable programming. Justice Breyer in his plurality opinion refused to define "a rigid single standard" for cable, stating that it would not be prudent to set a standard amidst all the "changes taking place in the law, the technology, and the industrial structure related to telecommunications."[39] This amounted to an explicit recognition of "changed circumstances," and gives further support to a private right to censor that would not rely on "single rigid standards" but would allow individuals the ability to regulate cable programming for themselves.

Continuing with the exclusive speaker-focus of *Denver Area*, the Court ruled in *Playboy Entertainment* that audiences must assume the full burden of avoiding unwanted or offensive speech.[40] *Playboy* involved a challenge to a provision in the Telecommunications Act of 1996 that required cable channels "primarily dedicated to sexually-oriented programming" to either "fully scramble or otherwise fully block" their channels or to limit their transmission to the hours between 10 p.m. and 6 p.m., when children are unlikely to be among the viewing audience.[41] Even before the enactment of this provision, cable operators used signal scrambling to limit programming access to paying customers. However, since this scrambling was imprecise and often led to signal bleed, the time-channeling regulation was intended to shield children from hearing or seeing images resulting from such signal bleed. Yet even though the Court recognized the strong state interest in shielding young viewers from such programming, it still struck down the law, holding that it constituted too great a burden on adult viewers.

In reaching its decision, the *Playboy* Court more or less assumed that a less restrictive alternative was available to parents who wished to keep their children from watching indecent programming.[42] This alternative required that the objecting parent request her cable operator to block any channel she did not wish to receive.[43] For this alternative to work, however, the cable operator would have to provide "adequate notice" to their subscribers that certain channels would broadcast sexually-oriented programming, that signal bleed may occur, that children might then see portions of the programming, and that parents should contact the cable operator to request a channel blocking device.[44] This notice, apparently, would be provided as an insert in the monthly cable bills.

Obviously, if the justices proposing this alternative saw it as reasonable and workable, they have never tried to contact their own cable operators. This was the point made in the dissent of Justice Breyer, who focused particularly on the issue of relative burdens. First, Justice Breyer noted that the law in question placed only a burden on adult programmers, not a ban. According to Justice Breyer, "adults may continue to watch adult channels, though less conveniently, by watching at night, recording programs with a VCR, or by subscribing to digital cable with better blocking systems."[45] Second, he observed that the law applies only to channels that "broadcast virtually 100% sexually explicit material."[46] And third, he recognized that because of signal bleed approximately 29 million children were exposed each year to sexually explicit programming. According to Justice Breyer, where over 28 million children have no parents at home after school, and where children may spend afternoons and evenings watching television outside of the home with friends, the time-channeling law offered "independent protection for a large number of families."[47] Given the compelling interest of child protection at issue, Justice Breyer concluded that the majority's proposed alternative was not at all an effective one.[48] In support of this conclusion, he cited evidence reflecting all the problems people had experienced in trying to get their cable operator to block certain channels—problems that come as no surprise to anyone who has ever tried to get their cable company to fix something.[49]

Reflecting the arguments in favor of a private right to censor, Justice Breyer argued that the First Amendment was not intended to leave millions of parents helpless in the face of media technologies that bring unwanted material into their children's lives.[50] Thus, according to Justice Breyer, an opt-in law may be just as valid as an opt-out law—for instance, a law requiring a person desiring adult programming to affirmatively direct that it be offered him, versus a law requiring someone not wanting adult programming to cause such programming to be blocked.

The *Playboy* decision reveals how the Court is placing great hope in technology to solve the problem of intrusive, unwanted speech.[51] According to the Court, the technological ability to block unwanted channels on a household-by-household basis "enables the Government to support parental authority without affecting the First Amendment interests of speakers and willing listeners."[52] The V-chip is an example of a technology meant to effectuate a private right of censorship.[53] But this faith in technology avoids the important constitutional issues posed by the private-right-to-censor theory. Furthermore, technology is no substitute for constitutional rights and doctrines. Evidence has shown, for instance, that various filtering technologies are far from perfect.[54] Moreover, many filtering technologies possess characteristics that inhibit their use. Lock boxes used to block out indecent cable programming, for example, require advance planning and thereby fail to protect those who scan from channel to channel and whose viewing of a given channel is unplanned and incomplete.

A new technology known as video-on-demand (VOD) promises to be more effective than the V-chip in preventing unwanted exposure to indecent programming and giving viewers total control over the programming that enters their homes. As a result, it promises to transform television from a "push" technology, in which control over what speech will be conveyed resides with media companies, into— at least in part—a "pull" technology, in which individuals decide for themselves which programs they would like to see.[55] Unfortunately, wide-scale deployment of VOD is not yet feasible. So at least until it is, and to combat the continuing onslaught of new media technologies that will keep shoving unwanted speech toward unwilling listeners, a private right to censor may be needed.

A Private Right to Censor as a Legislative Defense

A private right to censor would not qualify as a positive liberty, in the sense that it could be affirmatively asserted by each individual against any unwanted, nonpolitical speech. It would not give individuals the power to independently intervene in the communications marketplace so as to silence or alter certain media programming. A private right to censor can be no more powerful than the right to free speech, which under the First Amendment is a negative liberty that protects individuals "from" government interference with their speech freedoms. A positive liberty, on the other hand, affirmatively entitles individuals or society "to" a certain kind of speech or to a specific level of speech activities. As a negative liberty, a private right to censor would operate solely as a constitutional defense of governmental regulations seeking to facilitate such a right. It would provide a rights-based defense of the kind of programming restrictions at issue in *Playboy* and *Denver Area*, a defense that would obviously be stronger than a simple "social interests" defense.

Under a private-right-to-censor theory, elected legislatures would determine the types and forms of media speech that should be subject to private censorship rights. This speech would have to meet several conditions. First, it could not be political speech. Second, it would have to be speech that in its current form is intrusive, pervasive, and not easily avoided by unwilling listeners; it would have to be speech that unwilling recipients need some assistance in avoiding. Third, it would have to be speech in which society has a legitimate interest in helping unwilling audiences avoid. This "legitimate interest" would have to be established through legislative fact-finding, which in turn would identify specific individual and social harms caused by the speech; certainly, historic opposition to a particular kind of speech would be relevant. Most likely, the categories of speech subject to a private right to censor would include vulgarity, gratuitous violence, and indecent sexual speech.

This approach would allot to legislative bodies a freedom and flexibility that current First Amendment doctrines do not allow. It would give society's elected representatives a chance to help otherwise powerless individuals shape their own communicative interactions and environments. In a way, it would help achieve Justice Holmes' original intent regarding the achievement of social truth through acceptance in the democratic marketplace: For who better than a democratic body to determine social truth and the ways in which speech can best serve the goal of self-government? The role of the judiciary, then, would be to oversee this legislative process, and to make sure that the legislatures were adequately performing their duties and applying the least restrictive burdens on speech, given the needs of a private right to censor.

Notes

1. *Rowan v. United States Post Office*, 397 U.S. 728, 738 (1970) (stating that no one has a right to press even "good" ideas on an unwilling recipient).
2. *Miami Herald Publishing Co. v. Tornillo*, 418 U.S. 241, 258 (1974) (ruling that editing is a constitutionally protected function); *Hurley v. Irish-American Gay, Lesbian and Bisexual Group*, 515 U.S. 557, 573-4 (1995) (holding that the First Amendment protects the freedom to create one's own mix of speech).
3. *Rowan*, 397 U.S. 728, 735 (1970) (stating that people have "right to be let alone").
4. P. G. Ingram, *Censorship and Free Speech: Some Philosophical Bearings* (Burlington, VT: Ashgate Publishing Company, 2000), 119 (arguing that censorship is "a necessary accompaniment to free speech").
5. *Denver Area Educational Telecommunications Consortium v. F.C.C.*, 518 U.S. 727 (1996).
6. *National Endowment for the Arts v. Finley*, 524 U.S. 569 (1998).
7. *Advocates for the Arts v. Thomson*, 532 F.2d 792 (1st Cir. 1976).
8. Frederick Schauer, "The Ontology of Censorship," in *Censorship and Silencing*, Robert C. Post ed. (Los Angeles: The Getty Research Institute Publications and Exhibitions Program, 1995), 147.
9. Steven Heyman, "Ideological Conflict and the First Amendment," 78 *Chicago-Kent Law Review* 531, 599 (2003).
10. *American Medical Ass'n v. F.T.C.*, 638 F.2d 443 (2nd Cir. 1980); *Harper & Row v. Nation Enters*, 471 U.S. 539 (1985); *Associated Press v. United States*, 326 U.S. 1 (1945).
11. Rodney Smolla, *Smolla and Nimmer on Freedom of Speech* (Deerfield, IL: Clark Boardman Callahan, 2003), 4-2.
12. Jon. M. Garon, "Entertainment Law," 76 *Tulane Law Review* 559, 661 (2002).

13. See *Erznoznik v. Jacksonville*, 422 U.S. 205, 210 (1975) (striking down an ordinance prohibiting drive-in movie theaters from exhibiting nudity and holding that the burden falls upon the unwilling viewer to "avert [his] eyes").
14. *United States v. American Library Ass'n.*, 539 U.S. 194, (2003).
15. Ibid., 209.
16. *Lamont v. Postmaster General*, 381 U.S. 301, 305 (1965) (holding that the Post Office could not screen out communist mail from foreign sources and require potential recipients to request affirmatively its delivery (or opt-in); *Boler v. Youngs Drug Products Corp.*, 463 U.S. 60, 61 (1983) (holding that the federal government could not ban the unsolicited mailing of condom ads—a law which required opt-in).
17. *Reno*, 521 U.S. 844, 879 (1997).
18. Erika Hallace Kikuchi, "Spam in a Box," 10 *Boston University Journal of Science and Technology Law* 263 (2004).
19. Ibid., 285.
20. *Zelman v. Simmons-Harris*, 536 U.S. 639 (2002).
21. Steven Gey, "The Case Against Postmodern Censorship Theory," 145 *Univ. of Pennsylvania Law Review* 193, 232 (1996).
22. Alexander Meiklejohn, *Free Speech and Its Relation to Self-Government* (New York: Harper, 1948); Alexander Meiklejohn, *Political Freedom: The Constitutional Powers of the People* (New York: Oxford University Press, 1965).
23. Robert Post, "The Constitutional Status of Commercial Speech," 48 *UCLA Law Review* 1, 14-15 (2000).
24. *Dun & Bradstreet v. Greenmoss Builders, Inc.*, 472 U.S. 749, 758 (1985).
25. *F.C.C. v. Pacifica Foundation*, 438 U.S. 726 (1978).
26. Ibid., 748-9.
27. *Turner Broadcasting System, Inc. v. F.C.C.*, 520 U.S. 180 (1997).
28. *Pacifica*, 438 U.S. 726, 748.
29. *Turner Broadcasting System*, 520 U.S. 180 (1997).
30. Ibid., 228-29.
31. *Action for Children's Television v. F.C.C.*, 58 F.3d 654 (D.C. Cir. 1995).
32. Ibid., 661.
33. Ibid., 663.
34. Ibid., 667. The decision, however, only applied to broadcast television, not to cable.
35. *Dial Info. Svcs. v. Thornburgh*, 938 F.2d 1535 (2d Cir. 1991); *Info. Providers' Coalition v. FCC*, 928 F.2d 866 (9th Cir. 1991).
36. *Denver Area Educational Telecommunications v. F.C.C.*, 518 U.S. 727 (1996).
37. *New York Times v. U.S.*, 403 U.S. 713 (1971).
38. *Butler v. State of Michigan*, 352 U.S. 380, 383 (1957).
39. *Denver Area Educational Telecommunications*, 518 U.S. 727, 742.
40. *Playboy Entertainment Group, Inc.*, 529 U.S. 803, 813 (2000) (citing *Cohen v. California*, 403 U.S. 15, 21 (1971)).
41. Ibid., 806-7.
42. Ibid., 809.
43. Ibid., 810.
44. Ibid.
45. Ibid., 845.
46. Ibid., 839.
47. Ibid., 842.
48. Ibid., 841.
49. Ibid., 843.
50. Ibid., 846.

51.   Jennifer Polse, "United States v. Playboy Entertainment Group," 16 *Berkeley Technology Law Journal* 347, 348 (2001).
52.   *Playboy Entertainment Group, Inc.,* 529 U.S. 803, 815 (2000).
53.   J. M. Balkin, "Media Filters, the V-Chip, and the Foundations of Broadcast Regulation," 45 *Duke Law Journal* 1131, 1143 (1996).
54.   See Saul Hansell, "Agency Rebuffs a 'No E-Mail List,'" *New York Times*, June 16, 2004, A1.
55.   Christopher Yoo, "The Rise and Demise of the Technology-Specific Approach to the First Amendment," 91 *Georgetown Law Review* 245, 305 (2003).

4

Judicial Support for a Private Right to Censor

Although the courts have not expressly recognized a private right to censor as being protected by the First Amendment, an array of judicial decisions have laid a foundation for such a right. These cases have acknowledged the rights of listeners to avoid certain unwanted speech, and the courts have upheld governmental regulations supporting such rights, even when those regulations interfere with the freedoms of speakers.

The Captive Audience Doctrine

The Rights of Listeners Inside the Home

The Supreme Court has repeatedly protected the interests of unwilling listeners inside their own homes.[1] Within that space, a family's right to censor prevails over anyone else's right to speak. Despite "the value of exposing citizens to novel views, home is one place where a man ought to be able to shut himself up in his own ideas if he desires."[2] In *Rowan v. U.S. Post Office*,[3] the Court upheld a statute that strengthened homeowners' abilities to control what speech entered their homes. The statute permitted individuals, with the assistance of the postal service, to prevent the delivery of certain offensive mail. The Court conceded that the statute impeded the flow of ideas, but held that this effect was subordinate to the right of people in their homes "to be free from sights, sounds, and tangible matter we do not want." The Court also found that the law preserved individual autonomy by granting people some control over their exposure to offensive materials.[4]

Expanding on the rights of home-dwellers to shield themselves from unwanted speech, the Court, in a case involving the permissibility of restrictions on picketing in residential neighborhoods, ruled that protestors had "no right to force speech into the home of an unwilling listener."[5] The right to free speech, explained the Court, did not extend to speakers invading the privacy of residents who are essentially captives in their homes. Thus, where unwilling listeners are unable to repel intrusive speech from their homes without the aid of government regulations, speech rights must yield to listener rights; the First Amendment does not leave unwilling listeners help-less to endure the onslaught of offensive speech.

Generally, regulations assisting individuals in censoring unwanted speech coming into their homes are constitutional only if the unwanted speech comes from a single speaker, directed to a single recipient. These conditions are most purely met in the case of unwanted mail, since any censorship action by one recipient will not infringe upon anyone else's ability to receive the speech. However, in certain situa-tions the courts have upheld home censorship regulations even when those regulations affect speech flowing to the mass public rather than to specified individuals. Examples of such regulations include those that protect communities from auditory or visual clutter.[6]

In *Kovacs v. Cooper*, the Court upheld an ordinance prohibiting the use of sound trucks that emitted "loud and raucous noises," rea-soning that citizens in their homes should be protected from "aural aggression."[7] Although the statute essentially created a regulatory wall that blocked otherwise constitutionally protected speech, the Court noted that the "unwilling listener is practically helpless to es-cape this interference with his privacy by loud speakers except through the protection of the municipality."[8] It did not matter to the Court that not every person in the community wanted to keep out the information broadcast by the sound trucks, or that many persons might actually want to receive the information. The Court found it sufficient that "some" in the community found the sound trucks objectionable.[9] Likewise, in a later case, the Court sustained a regu-lation designed to prevent the disturbance of nearby residents by requiring that music performers in a Central Park band shell use a sound system provided by the city.[10]

Even though courts have been more willing to be listener- or au-dience-focused when the unwanted speech is occurring within the home, the influence of the marketplace model has hardly waned. In *Bolger v. Youngs Drug Products Corp.*, for instance, the Court struck down a federal law that banned the mailing of unsolicited advertise-ments for contraceptives.[11] Though acknowledging the privacy interest in the home and the interest of parents in shielding their children from objectionable materials, the Court concluded that parents can easily police a mailbox.[12] According to the *Bolger* Court, the short journey from the mailbox to the trash can is an acceptable burden on the right to avoid offensive material.[13] Thus, even in one's home, offensive speech can still be governed by an opt-out scheme that places all the burdens on unwilling recipients. It does not matter that the tens of millions of working parents may not be able to adequately police the mailbox; nor does it matter that such information is plentiful in the marketplace of ideas and that there are so many other available avenues for obtaining such information.

Under a private right to censor, however, a *Bolger*-type regulation could very well be sustained, particularly if it is legislatively found that such materials are offensive to a significant number of people. First, contraceptive advertisements are non-political speech. Second, this information is plentiful in the contemporary marketplace of ideas. Third, there are numerous avenues through which to obtain information on contraceptives. Consequently, it should not be unconstitutional to shift the burden of avoiding this information away from home residents and onto people desiring it. In other words, an opt-in scheme should be allowed, with those wishing to receive such information given the burden of requesting it.

The Rights of Captive Audiences Outside the Home

Although the courts have been most sensitive to listener rights inside the home, they have also recognized the rights of captive audiences outside the home to be free of unwanted speech. Overall, the captive audience doctrine has not exerted a prevalent influence in First Amendment jurisprudence, nor has it significantly challenged the marketplace model. Even though it has been the only area in which there has been any real judicial recognition of the unwilling listener, the doctrine seems more a recognition of some right of privacy than of any right of private censorship. (Although, in the media society that America has become, there is an argument that the entire public has become a captive audience.)

Some recent cases, however, seem to be reviving the doctrine, recognizing that "changed circumstances" may warrant its application. As Professor Balkin argues, the captive audience doctrine should not focus solely on the home, but "should regulate particular situations where people are particularly subject to [unwanted speech]."[14]

Lehman v. City of Shaker Heights[15] is a leading case on the captive audience doctrine. In *Lehman*, finding that streetcar riders are a captive audience, the Court upheld restrictions on material that could be played over a speaker system in public transit vehicles.[16] As the Court recognized, individuals riding in a moving vehicle for an extended period of time are unable to avoid objectionable speech. Of course, they could have walked to work or kept their ears plugged while taking the public transit, but the Court did not require them to go to those extremes so as to "avert their eyes." In a more recent decision relying upon *Lehman* and upholding the authority of a public transit commission to ban advertisements for the legalization of marijuana, the court stated that "it would be unacceptable" to subject "captive audiences of commuters, tourists, and schoolchildren to all sorts of graphic advertisements that could not be regulated for content."[17]

In the past, the courts have often shied away from the captive audience doctrine because the unwilling listener or viewer could fairly easily avert their eyes from the offensive speech. If a drive-in movie theater was playing a movie with offensive scenes in it, one could avoid driving by it during the two hours that the movie was playing. If a speaker in a town park was yelling out offensive speech, one could cross the street and walk the other way. But it is quite another matter with the Internet. If it is as easy as the Court in *American Library Ass'n* says it is to access indecent speech on the Internet, and if there is no way for parents to adequately site- or content-block, and if the Internet is indeed an integral part of contemporary life, then is it even feasible to expect people to avert their eyes to all the sexually explicit speech that pops up on the Internet? Captivity can be measured in many different ways. To parents of young children gaining access to sexually explicit material online, it doesn't matter if the captivity is of the child's own doing—namely, that of turning on the computer and clicking the mouse—it just matters that their children are in fact being held captive by an unwelcome intruder.

The Internet has essentially erased the boundaries between public and private spaces.[18] It can be accessed anywhere. Therefore, the captive audience doctrine should not focus on particular spaces like the home; rather, it should regulate "particular situations where people are particularly subject to unwanted speech."[19] Captivity in this sense is about the right not to have to flee, rather than the inability to flee.[20] With regard to the Internet, perhaps the doctrine is about parents not always having to be on guard, every second of their children's usage. Perhaps it is about not having to ban all Internet use by their children because of the impracticalities or impossibilities of constant monitoring. As Professor Nachbar notes, not only do very few parents have the time to supervise all the time that their children spend on the Internet, but "unless the parent were, for example, to open each [web] page with the child looking away and only allow the child to view the page after a parental preview, there is no way to keep the child from taking in the content while the parent is evaluating its appropriateness."[21]

In modern society, accessing the Internet has become a basic function of everyday life, as much as having to commute to work on city buses or having to walk past an adult theater on the way to school. Therefore, children at a computer screen should be seen as a captive audience—being where they have every right to be, where they have to be in terms of their educational development, and where their parents really have no way of effectively shielding them from unwanted or offensive images or material. In *Bethel School District v. Fraser*, the Court recognized the state's legitimate desire "to protect children—especially in a captive audience—from exposure to sexually explicit, indecent, or lewd speech."[22]

Prior to the Internet, it was easier to segregate sexually explicit speech away from children.[23] Adult theaters and bookstores could restrict entry to anyone without a valid ID. Stores that sold adult magazines could stock those magazines behind the counter or place them in sealed plastic bags, prohibiting access to children.[24] In *American Booksellers Association v. Webb*, for instance, a statute was upheld that banned the display in any public place where minors might be present of materials "harmful to minors."[25] In connection with the regulation of indecent materials, states could follow a two-pronged approach.[26] First, they could use zoning laws to regulate the location of "adult-oriented establishments."[27] Second, they could require an age identification to enter those establishments. But in the electronic world of the Internet, these methods for regulating minor's access to indecency are ineffective or nonexistent.[28] Even though some adult-material websites charge for access to their sites, children can get a healthy dose of the material before they are ever required to input a credit card number.[29] Therefore, through the Internet, children can access material that state pornography laws prohibit them from purchasing at retail stores.

American Library Ass'n can be seen as laying the parameters of a captive audience doctrine applicable to the Internet. Children are just as captive in front of a computer screen at the library as in front of a television screen at home. And, given the realities of modern life, they could be spending as much of their after-school hours at a library or community center or friend's house as at home. In *Action for Children's Television v. FCC*, the court emphasized the impossibility of real parental control over what television broadcasting their children saw, and reaffirmed that the government "has an independent and compelling interest in preventing minors from being exposed to indecent broadcasts."[30] This same analysis would also apply to the ability to supervise computer use. In fact, given the speed with which one can access and exit Internet sites, it is most likely more difficult to supervise computer use than television viewing.

Intrusive Technology and the Rights of Listeners

Freedom from Broadcast Indecency

Perhaps the most prominent example of listener-based restrictions on speech directed to a mass audience involves FCC regulations on indecent broadcast programming. Similar to the speech in *Kovacs*, television programming constitutes speech emanating from a single source and directed to a large audience of listeners. Yet in *Pacifica*, the Court upheld FCC rules restricting the broadcast of indecent material to hours when children would less likely be in the audience.[31] The justifications for this ruling were twofold. First, the regulations were necessary because of the pervasive presence of broadcast media in American life. Relying on the captive audience doctrine, the Court stated that indecent broadcast material confronts the individual in the privacy of her own home, where the right "to be left alone plainly outweighs the First Amendment rights of an intruder."[32] Second, the Court found that broadcasting "is uniquely accessible to children, even those too young to read."[33] Thus, channeling indecent material into hours when children were unlikely to be listening was the only effective way of shielding children from such material.

Stressing the need to preserve the home as a sanctuary, safe from unwanted speech or images, the *Pacifica* Court compared the broadcast audience to the *Kovacs* home-dwellers who were unable to escape the loudspeaker intrusion. Consequently, like the *Kovacs* home-dwellers, broadcast listeners and viewers also needed some government protection, since he or she could tune into the middle of a program and without warning be exposed to offensive, indecent speech.

Prior to *Pacifica*, the Supreme Court had stated that it is "the right of the viewers and listeners, not the right of the broadcasters, which is paramount."[34] This listener-focus, in contrast to the marketplace model's exclusively speaker-centered view of the First Amendment, appeared again in Justice Breyer's plurality opinion in *Denver Area*.[35] Justice Breyer stated that the *Pacifica* rationales—pervasiveness, invasion of the home, ineffectiveness of warnings, accessibility to children—applied with equal force to cable television, thus justifying a less protective level of scrutiny than that typically associated with content-based regulation.[36] In terms of intrusiveness and pervasiveness, Breyer found little difference between cable and broadcast television. Justice Breyer even implied that *Pacifica* might extend to all media, noting that the question of whether "*Pacifica* does, or does not, impose some lesser standard of review where indecent speech is at issue" is still open.[37]

Freedom from Intrusive Technologies

The courts have upheld regulations on offensive speech that apply across the board, not just individually on a home-by-home basis. Both the Second and Ninth Circuits, for instance, have sustained restrictions on access to dial-a-porn services, finding that such restrictions were necessary to protect the children of parents who did not wish them to hear this particular kind of speech.[38]

Through the captive audience doctrine, courts have given increased importance to listener rights regarding certain new technologies. In *Bland v. Fessler*,[39] the court upheld a restriction on telemarketers' use of automatic dialing and announcing devices (ADADs). It ruled that ADADs were much more disruptive than door-to-door solicitors, and "more of a nuisance and a greater invasion of privacy than telemarketing with live operators."[40] The court then held that the regulation at issue did not amount to an absolute ban on speech, since the use of ADADs were permitted so long as the called party consented to the message (although it is difficult to imagine that many people would ever so consent). The court also found that a do-not call list was not a less restrictive means of accomplishing the government's objective, since such a list would place the burden on the public to stop disruptive ADAD calls from arriving at their homes. Nor did the court accept the argument that people should be left to themselves to combat ADADs, by turning off their ringers or screening their calls or simply hanging up on the prerecorded calls.[41] In other words, the court did not impose an "averting one's eye's" burden on the recipients of the calls; it did not place all the burden on the recipient to opt-out.

Similar to a private right to censor, the *Bland* decision recognizes that in a world pervaded by media technologies, the captive audience doctrine can have a wider application in First Amendment jurisprudence. As the Supreme Court once observed, because of "constantly proliferating new and ingenious forms of expression, we are inescapably captive audiences for many purposes."[42] Communications technologies are continually exposing people to new kinds of unwanted speech. Sitting in the computer section of the library, a person can glance around and see the screen of someone else as they view a sexually graphic website. Television programs prohibited by parents are graphically advertised during other programs. Huge video screens run day and night in public places. Internet terminals are waiting and ready in coffee houses and even fast-food restaurants.

The captive audience doctrine is based on the belief that people should have some privacy from exposure to unwanted speech. And if privacy is a constitutional right, why should it be completely subservient to the speech rights of speakers? If people have a privacy right to go to a store and buy contraceptives, shouldn't they have a privacy right to exclude unwanted media sources from influencing their children's sexual development?

Revisionist Opinions About the Internet

Up until *American Library Ass'n*, the courts had generally expressed a very optimistic vision of the Internet. In *Blumenthal v. Drudge*, the court glowingly described the Internet as enabling "people to communicate with one another with unprecedented speed and efficiency," representing "an extraordinary advance in the availability of educational and informational resources to our citizens."[43] The court stated that the Internet should remain unregulated so as "to maintain the robust nature of Internet communication."[44] Earlier, in *Zeran*, a negligence action brought against an Internet service provider, the court upheld judgment for the provider, stating that the Internet has "flourished, to the benefit of all Americans."[45]

But the landmark Internet case was *Reno v. ACLU*, in which the Court struck down provisions in the Communications Decency Act of 1996 that prohibited the Internet transmission of indecent messages to anyone under eighteen years of age.[46] In its decision, the Court described the nature of the Internet:

> The Web is thus comparable, from the readers' viewpoint, to both a vast library including millions of readily available and indexed publications and a sprawling mall offering goods and services. From the publishers' point of view, it constitutes a vast platform from which to address and hear from a worldwide audience of millions of readers, viewers, researchers and buyers. Any person or organization with a computer connected to the Internet can publish information.[47]

Although recognizing the presence of sexually explicit material on the Internet, the Court found that "users seldom encounter such content accidentally."[48] With pornographic material normally preceded by warnings as to its content, the Court concluded that "the odds are slim that a user would enter a sexually explicit site by accident."[49] Unlike television or radio, according to the Court, a child requires "some sophistication and some ability to...retrieve material and thereby use the Internet unattended."[50]

These optimistic views of the Internet have been echoed by scholars and commentators.[51] Even in a decision predating *American Library Ass'n* by just one year, the Supreme Court described the Internet as "a forum for a true diversity of political discourse, unique opportunities for cultural development, and myriad avenues for intellectual activity."[52] However, in *Ashcroft,* the Court did begin to back off from its earlier view in *Reno*, finding that children could access Internet pornography simply "by stumbling upon [it]."[53]

Crucial to the Court's holding in *American Library Ass'n* was the finding that children could unintentionally be exposed to sexually explicit material on the Internet.[54] By this time, national surveys had showed that a quarter of all school children had inadvertently downloaded pornography while at a public library.[55] This finding coincided with other studies that had been conducted on Internet pornography.[56] As the *Washington Post* described it, the Internet was "the largest pornography store in history."[57] And contrary to the Court's implication in *Reno*, studies found that most children "demonstrate a computer proficiency that far surpasses that of their parents" and generally have little problem finding whatever material they want on the Internet.[58] Adolescents between the ages of twelve and seventeen have been cited as one of the largest consumers of adult-oriented material on the Internet.[59] Consequently, by the time *American Library Ass'n* came to the Court, there had evolved a realization of all the ways in which the *Reno* Court was wrong in its view of indecency on the Internet.

Despite requiring a credit card for access, most pornography sites offer extensive free previews, thereby allowing children to see graphic sexual and violent images without going through any age verification process.[60] Furthermore, even though many pornographic sites carry disclaimers, warning viewers that the material contains sexually explicit images, "these disclaimers are about as effective as constructing a retaining wall out of tissue paper."[61] In addition, search engines have made it even easier for inexperienced users to find sexually explicit websites; and because Internet searches take only a few seconds, they can easily be executed by a student in a classroom while the teacher is in a different part of the room, and the student can exit the site in a matter of seconds if an authority figure approaches. And finally, with approximately 40 percent of Internet content originating from foreign sources, domestic laws alone cannot keep pornography from getting on the Internet and to the attention of children.[62]

Unquestionably, the Internet is a democratizing medium, offering anyone with a computer the ability to speak and share her opinions. But it is also capable of conveying an almost unlimited amount of hate, pornography, violence, and vulgarity.[63] Contrary to the *Reno* Court's assumptions, it is not difficult or complicated for children to log on to the Internet; nor is it difficult to find sites dedicated to pornography and violence.[64]

The Internet is no replica of eighteenth-century town meetings, in which people openly shared and debated opinions. One big difference with the Internet is its anonymity feature.[65] Speech can take on an entirely different character when it is being conducted anonymously, and it can more easily lead to the dangers of stalking, deception, and manipulation. During the eighteenth century, taking public responsibility for one's speech necessarily imposed some constraints on that speech.[66] A sort of social custom and decorum served to censor out the more violent or crude statements. But today, with the Internet, there is no social custom available. There is nothing except for the user's own ability to censor unwanted, offensive speech. Given these conditions, the courts may be more willing to consider applying to the Internet a *Pacifica*-type approach that gives added weight to user and viewer interests.

The Rights of Unwilling Listeners in Public

Where Listener Rights Supercede Speaker Rights

If a free communicative process is at the heart of the First Amendment, then listener protections should apply equally in public as well as in the home, especially since in a media-filled world the boundaries of "home" are less important and less definable than they once were. And even though the articulation of listener rights poses a serious challenge, since a fine line separates such rights from overt state censorship, the courts have nonetheless provided some direction in this regard.

One area of case law in which the courts have given precedence to listener rights in connection with public speech has involved the regulation of offensive art confronting an unsuspecting viewer. In *Close v. Lederle*,[67] for instance, the court found that a display of sexually explicit paintings in the corridor of a university's student union amounted to an "assault upon individual privacy." A similar finding in another case justified the relocation of a prominent display of "sexually explicit and racially offensive art."[68] Likewise, a "vulgar, shocking and tasteless painting" was removed on the grounds that it "was displayed in the direct line of vision of everyone who entered the Federal Courthouse."[69] Yet, even aside from vulgarity and offensiveness, courts have upheld listener rights in the removal or diminishment of speech that over-clutters the public domain. In *Members of the City Council of the City of Los Angeles v. Taxpayers for Vincent*, the Court found that a municipal ordinance prohibiting the posting of signs on public property was not unconstitutional even as applied to political campaign speech. While acknowledging that the ordinance diminished the total quantity of speech, the Court ruled that it was justified by the city's interest in maintaining the aesthetic appeal of the community.[70]

Listeners or viewers have also been given freedom from offensive speech in certain employment situations. This "trumping" of speech rights by listener rights occurred in a lawsuit brought by a female employee who felt offended and harassed by the presence of "girlie calendars, pornographic centerfolds and sexual graphic cartoons" in the workplace.[71] The employer asserted a free speech defense, alleging that the offensive materials were protected by the First Amendment. But the court rejected this defense, holding that the pictures were not protected speech, since they created an abusive working environment.

Privacy and the Freedom from Unwanted Speech

Privacy concerns have been rising as the information age progresses. Credit card companies and health care providers have been restricted in their speech rights regarding customers and patients. Telemarketers have come under intense scrutiny from a public that is weary of having its privacy invaded. Throughout society, there is a growing desire to create a privacy zone free of media intrusion, and especially of media speech that pierces into the most personal areas of human life.

Courts have recognized a right to privacy, even in public places.[72] In *Kramer v. Downey*, the court stated that "we now hold that the right to privacy is broad enough to include the right to be free of those willful intrusions into one's personal life at home and at work which occurred in this case."[73] And in *Dietermann v. Time, Inc.*, involving an invasion of privacy action against the press, the court declared that though freedom of speech and press are constitutional guarantees, so is the right of privacy.[74]

The evolution of a constitutional right of privacy has occurred primarily in the area of human sexuality: *Griswold v. Connecticut*[75] involved the right to purchase contraceptives; *Roe v. Wade*[76] involved the right to an abortion; and *Lawrence v. Texas*[77] involved the right to engage in homosexual sex. These cases have established that people have a right to develop and practice their own sexuality in private, without the intervention of others. And yet, given the prevalence of sex in today's media, children and adolescents who are exposed to such images and attitudes are having their sexual development (perhaps the most personal area of human development) shaped by an anonymous media.[78] Sexually explicit speech, by exposing children to ideas or images that are repugnant to the parents' beliefs, can invade a parent's privacy right to familial autonomy. As Justice Brennan once postulated, the right of privacy includes not only the freedom of choice regarding the upbringing of children, but the "autonomous control over the development and expression of one's intellect and personality," free from interference by others.[79] Furthermore, as emphasized by the briefs in *Griswold*, married couples ought not be forced to choose between abstinence and the consequences of pregnancy, since given the realities of the human sex drive abstinence is not possible for most couples.[80] Likewise, given the realities of the modern media age, avoidance of offensive, intrusive speech is not possible for most people.

In connection with the prevalence and intrusiveness of unwanted media speech, an increasing sensitivity to privacy has somewhat reinvigorated the captive audience doctrine and made courts more receptive to listener rights. The most sweeping decision linking privacy rights with the captive audience doctrine occurred in *Hill v. Colorado*, where the Supreme Court recognized an individual's right to privacy from the unwanted intrusion of speech, even when that individual is in a public venue.[81]

In *Hill*, the Court upheld a Colorado statute creating a "floating buffer zone" that prohibited anyone from coming within eight feet of another person, outside of an abortion clinic and without that person's consent, for the purpose of passing out a leaflet or engaging in oral protest or counseling. The Court recognized that the law imposed burdens on the ability of protestors to speak to people entering or leaving the clinic.[82] It also recognized that the speech of the protestors was protected by the First Amendment, and that the public streets and sidewalks that were covered by the statute were "quintessential" public forums for free speech.[83] Yet the Court emphasized the "significant difference between state restrictions on a speaker's right to address a willing audience and those that protect listeners from unwanted communication."[84] It also noted that the protection normally afforded to offensive speech would not always apply when the unwilling audience was unable to avoid the speech. In elaborating on the "right to be left alone," the Court stated that the case law has "repeatedly recogniz[ed] the interests of unwilling listeners in situations where the degree of captivity makes it impractical for the unwilling viewer to avoid exposure."[85] Thus, in the Court's opinion, people can be "captives" to speech even outside the sanctuary of their homes and in ways that can justify governmental regulation of offensive speech. According to the Court, the rights of the listener to be free of offensive speech "must be placed in the scales with the right of others to communicate."[86]

The dissent argued that "the right to be left alone" was a right that was only conferred as against the government, and not as against private protestors.[87] It asserted that the governmental interest in protecting people from unwanted communications had never before been extended to speech on public sidewalks. The dissent also argued that the speech burdens imposed on the protestors were significant.[88] Eight feet is not a normal conversational distance, the dissent claimed, especially when the goal is not to protest but to engage in counseling and educating—activities that cannot be done at a distance and at a high-decibel level.[89] The availability of bullhorns and loudspeakers, as the majority proposed, would be of "little help to the woman who hopes to forge, in the last moments before another of her sex is to have an abortion, a bond of concern and intimacy that might enable her to persuade the woman to change her mind and heart."[90] Furthermore, the dissent argued, "it does not take a veteran labor organizer to recognize that leafletting will be rendered utterly ineffectual by a requirement that the leafleter obtain from each subject permission to approach. That simply is not how it is done, and the Court knows it."[91]

Even though the burdens on speech caused by the Colorado statute were significant, the Court ruled in favor of the privacy interests of people in a public forum wishing to be shielded from the speech of other individuals. It adopted an unwilling-listener focus to the First Amendment, rather than the speaker-focus of the marketplace model. Thus, under the holding in *Hill*, it cannot be said that the burdens caused by a private right to censor would be unconstitutional.

Despite the speech at issue in *Hill* being clearly political speech, the Court still designated protection of the rights of unwilling listeners as a governmental interest sufficient to justify restrictions on that speech. Moreover, the Court left open the possibility that the protection of unwilling listeners could be interpreted not just as a significant governmental interest, but as a compelling one that could justify significant content-based restrictions on any kind of speech. Thus, the *Hill* ruling actually went further than does the proposed private right to censor.

In the wake of *Hill*, and under a private-right-to-censor-theory, it can be argued that *Erznoznik v. City of Jacksonville* was wrongly decided.[92] That case involved a city ordinance that prohibited films containing nudity from being shown at drive-in theaters where the screen could be seen from the street. The rationale for the ordinance was one of protecting motorists, who were essentially a captive audience, from seeing images that would be offensive. But the Court denied this rationale, completely ignoring the rights of unwilling viewers whose privacy interests were violated by objectionable speech. Contrary to *Hill*, the *Erznoznik* Court placed all the burdens on the unwilling viewer to avoid the speech.

Not only does *Hill* seem to reverse prior case law that refused to apply the captive audience doctrine in public forums, but it could also be seen as the beginnings of a new privacy right that might serve as a counterweight to the otherwise unrestricted speech rights of others. At the very least, however, *Hill* suggests that there are cases in which the state has an interest in assisting an unwilling listener to avoid unwanted speech, even in public forums. This means that "the constitutional rule that allows the government to enforce individuals' decisions not to receive these types of information exists despite the fact that it potentially precludes some communicative interaction."[93] And this is precisely the premise of a private right to censor.

Under *Hill*, the captive audience doctrine is expanded from a focus simply on the physical location of the listener to a broader view of the speech harms sought to be eliminated. In other words, mere physical location should not be constitutionally determinative; instead, the privacy interests of the listener should be the controlling factor. As Professor Heyman argues, "the right of individuals to be free from unwanted exposure to sexual material should apply not only in the private but also in the public sphere."[94] The freedom not to view intrusive and offensive sexual material should not exist only when one is safely within the confines of home. Individuals "who are in public places should have a right to enjoy the public environment and to participate in the life of the community without averting their eyes from intensely personal matter that they do not wish to see."[95]

Judicial Protection of the Upbringing of Children

In almost every case involving indecent speech, the courts address the most obvious purpose of any attempted restrictions on such speech: that of the protection of children. The courts have gone to great length to carve out special constitutional protections for children.[96] But this concern with shielding minors from indecent speech often erodes when it comes in conflict with the speech rights of adults and the interests of the marketplace model. Few measures shielding minors from indecent speech are upheld if they have any restraining effect on the ability of adults to access such speech.[97] Consequently, the child protection interest frequently loses out to the abundance goal, to the idea that any burden on speech is the equivalent of an unconstitutional infringement.

Despite this advantage enjoyed by the marketplace model, however, courts have recognized that society has a strong interest in enabling parents to raise their children according to their personal beliefs. Courts, for instance, have upheld laws prohibiting the distribution of pornographic materials to children under a particular age, preventing children from obtaining abortions without parental notification, and precluding persons under a certain age from purchasing alcohol and cigarettes.[98] Because of the importance of the childrearing process, the constitutional demands of free speech must be "applied with sensitivity...to the special needs of parents and children."[99] The Supreme Court has specifically ruled that government has an interest in facilitating parental control over what their children see and hear.[100] This interest seeks to empower parents' right to control the communications environment of their children and to direct their children's education as they see fit.[101]

But in addition to this interest in empowering parental childrearing, the government possesses an independent interest in the mental and emotional development of children into mature citizens, regardless of the decisions made by their parents.[102] As the Supreme Court has stated, a democratic government requires "the healthy, well-rounded growth of young people into full maturity as citizens, with all that implies."[103] This governmental interest also includes the inculcation of certain civic values that in turn will mold individual character so as to instill a sense of public duty and public good.[104] One way to achieve this character development is to prevent childhood exposure to harmful speech and images.[105] Consequently, where children are involved, freedoms of speech may have to be "balanced against society's countervailing interest in teaching the boundaries of socially appropriate behavior."[106] This balancing has justified, for instance, the restriction of sexually graphic speech expressed during a high school assembly.[107]

The Court has ruled that speech protected by the First Amendment as to adults may not necessarily be protected as to children. In *Ginsberg v. New York*, a statute prohibiting the sale to minors of otherwise constitutionally protected pornography was upheld.[108] The Court declared that the governmental interest in protecting the well-being of children is not limited to protecting them from physical and psychological harm, but also extends to protecting them from material that may impair their ethical and moral development.[109] Even though the *Ginsberg* Court doubted the scientific certainty of the legislative conclusion that the material banned by the statute did in fact impair the ethical and moral development of children, it noted that such a link had not been disproved.[110] This same approach was taken in *ACT III*, where the court, in upholding broadcast decency regulations, stated that "a scientific demonstration of psychological harm is [not] required in order to establish the constitutionality of measures protecting minors from exposure to indecent speech."[111]

The majority of parents strongly support the "efforts of Congress to protect children from harmful" and offensive entertainment speech.[112] According to congressional findings, the average child witnesses approximately 10,000 acts of violence on television by the time that child completes elementary school.[113] There are many who believe that a community should have the authority to protect children from exposure to this kind of media output, and that the "widespread availability of such material in the larger society makes it virtually impossible for parents to act effectively on their own."[114] Yet most attempts to do so have been foiled by the courts' one-sided application of the First Amendment.

In addressing the problem of access to pornography on the Internet, Congress has tried on several occasions to construct doorways that will seal off sexually explicit material from children. In 1996, it passed the Communications Decency Act, which prohibited the transmission over the Internet of indecent material to anyone under the age of 18.[115] This prohibition, however, was struck down as unconstitutional in *Reno*.[116] Next, Congress passed the Child Online Protection Act ("COPA").[117] This statute forbad any person from using the World Wide Web to make "any communication for commercial purposes that is available to any minor and that includes any material that is harmful to minors."[118] But the Court struck down this law in *Ashcroft v. ACLU*.[119] Then, with the Child Pornography and Prevention Act, Congress expanded the federal prohibition on child pornography to include computer-generated images of minors engaging in sexually explicit conduct ("virtual child pornography").[120] Again, this law was overturned in *Ashcroft v. Free Speech Coalition*.[121]

In *Reno*, the Court agreed that there is "a compelling interest in protecting the physical and psychological well-being of minors, which extended to shielding them from indecent messages."[122] However, as the Court has done on so many previous occasions, it downgraded this interest when it conflicted with the rights of adults to access, burden-free, such messages.

Adhering to the marketplace model, the courts have denied efforts to regulate indecent speech accessible to children, relying on the principle that in seeking to protect youth the government cannot "reduce the adult population...to reading only what is fit for children."[123] But this ignores reality: that so much of the violent and sexually graphic speech today is aimed not at adults but at children. Furthermore, by adhering so steadfastly to the marketplace model, courts often make a cursory rejection of the government's proffered rationale for regulations infringing on the burden-free access to indecent speech.[124]

Ironically, the courts seem to be far more eager to repress non-entertainment forms of speech for the sake of protecting children. In *Bering v. SHARE*, for instance, the Washington Supreme Court found that the state's compelling interest in protecting children from disturbing speech justified an injunction limiting the speech of anti-abortion picketers. This injunction applied to the use of words such as "murder," "kill," and "their derivatives" during demonstrations outside a medical building where abortions were performed.[125]

A greater focus on listener rights, as well as a stronger First Amendment recognition of the right of parents to control their family's communicative environment, would greatly help society in protecting children from harmful speech. As one court has admitted, "It is fanciful to believe that the vast majority of parents who wish to shield their children from indecent material can effectively do so without meaningful restrictions on the airing of broadcast indecency."[126] One way of assisting parents, while at the same time not imposing a complete prohibition on adult's access to such speech, is to enact legislation empowering a private right to censor.

Notes

1. *Frisby v. Schultz*, 487 U.S. 474, 484 (1988) (describing the home as a hallowed sanctuary, where individuals are entitled to respite from the bombardments of social life); *United States v. On Lee*, 193 F.2d 306, 316 (2d Cir. 1951) (a "sane, decent society must provide some...oasis, some insulated enclosure, some enclave, some inviolate place which is a man's castle").
2. *Hynes v. Mayor of Oradell*, 425 U.S. 610, 619 (1976).
3. *Rowan v. U.S. Post Office*, 397 U.S. 728, 736 (1970).
4. Ibid.
5. *Frisby v. Schultz*, 487 U.S. 474, 485 (1988).
6. *Ward v. Rock Against Racism*, 491 U.S. 781, 792 (1989); *Metromedia, Inc. v. City of San Diego*, 453 U.S. 490, 507 (1981).
7. *Kovacs v. Cooper*, 336 U.S. 77 (1949).

8.   Ibid., 86-87.
9.   Ibid., 102, 81.
10. *Ward*, 491 U.S. 781 (1989).
11. *Bolger v. Youngs Drug Products Corp.*, 463 U.S. 60 (1983).
12. Ibid., 74.
13. Ibid., 72
14. J. M. Balkin, "Free Speech and Hostile Environments," 99 *Columbia Law Review* 2295, 2312 (1999).
15. *Lehman v. City of Shaker Heights*, 418 U.S. 298, 307 (1974).
16. *Young v. American Mini-Theaters*, 427 U.S. 50, 63 (1976) (finding that the neighborhood constituted a captive audience); *Unites States v. Kokinda*, 497 U.S. 720 (1990) (upholding a postal service regulation that prohibited political and commercial solicitation on a sidewalk near a post office entrance, after the state had asserted an interest in protecting).
17. *Change The Climate, Inc. v. MBTA*, 214 F.Supp.2d 125, 133 (D. Mass. 2002).
18. Kathleen M. Sullivan, "First Amendment Intermediaries in the Age of Cyberspace," 45 *U.C.L.A. Law Review* 1653, 1675 (1998); Balkin, "Free Speech," 2311.
19. Balkin, "Free Speech," 2312.
20. Ibid.
21. Thomas Nachbar, "Paradox and Structure: Relying on Government Regulation to Preserve the Internet's Unregulated Character," 85 *Minnesota Law Review* 215, 220-1 (2000).
22. *Bethel School Dist. No. 403 v. Fraser*, 474 U.S. 675, 684 (1986) (upholding a school's restriction on an indecent speech at a school assembly).
23. *Ginsberg v. New York*, 390 U.S. 629 (1968) (upholding a law that restricted the distribution even of printed matter to children, thereby establishing the rule that the government can adapt more stringent controls on communicative materials available to youths than on those available to adults).
24. *Crawford v. Lungren*, 96 F.3d 380, 382 (9th Cir. 1996) (finding no constitutional violation with a statute seeking to prevent exposing minors to indecent material, which banned the sale of "harmful matter" from unsupervised, sidewalk vending machines, unless identification cards were required).
25. *American Booksellers v. Webb*, 919 F.2d 1493, 1512 (11th Cir. 1990) (the suit challenging the Georgia law having been brought by a group of booksellers and publishers).
26. *Reno*, 521 U.S. 844, 889 (1997) (O'Connor, J., dissenting in part, concurring in part).
27. Elizabeth M. Shea, "The Children's Internet Protection Act of 1999: Is Internet Filtering Software the Answer?" 24 *Seton Hall Legislative Journal* 167, 172 (1999).
28. Glenn E. Simon, "Cyberporn and Censorship: Constitutional Barriers to Preventing Access to Internet Pornography by Minors," 88 *Journal of Criminal Law & Criminology* 1015, 1043 (1998).
29. Ibid.
30. *Action for Children's Television v. FCC*, 58 F.3d 654, 663 (D.C. Cir. 1995).
31. *F.C.C. v. Pacifica Foundation*, 438 U.S. 726 (1978).
32. Ibid., 748.
33. Ibid., 749.
34. *Red Lion Broadcasting Co. v. F.C.C.*, 395 U.S. 367, 390 (1969).
35. *Denver Area Educational Telecommunications Consortium, Inc. v. F.C.C.*, 518 U.S. 727 (1996).
36. Ibid., 744-45.

37. Ibid., 755.
38. *Dial Information Svcs. v. Thornburgh*, 938 F.2d 1535 (2d Cir. 1991); *Information Providers' Coalition v. FCC*, 928 F.2d 866 (9th Cir. 1991).
39. *Bland and Fessler,* 88 F.3d 729, 731 (9th Cir. 1996) (upholding a California law prohibiting the use of automatic dialing and announcing devices unless a live operator first identified the calling party and obtained the called party's consent to listen to the prerecorded message).
40. Ibid., 733.
41. Ibid., 736.
42. *Erznoznik v. City of Jacksonville*, 422 U.S. 205, 210-11 (1975).
43. *Blumenthal v. Drudge,* 992 F. Supp. 44, 48 (D.D.C. 1998).
44. Ibid., 50.
45. *Zeran v. America Online, Inc.,* 129 F.3d 327, 330 (4th Cir. 1997); *Ashcroft v. American Civil Liberties Union*, 535 U.S. 564, 566 (2002) (recognizing that the "Internet...offers a forum for a true diversity of political discourse, unique opportunities for cultural development, and myriad avenues for intellectual activity"); *Cubby Inc. v. CompuServe, Inc.*, 776 F. Supp. 135, 140 (S.D.N.Y. 1991) (stating that the Internet is "at the forefront of the information...revolution...[making it possible] for an individual with a personal computer...to have instantaneous access to thousands of news publications from across the United States and around the world").
46. *Reno*, 521 U.S. 844 (1997); 47 U.S.C. § 223(a) and (d).
47. *Reno*, 521 U.S. 844, 853 (1997).
48. Ibid., 854.
49. Ibid.
50. Ibid.
51. For optimistic outlooks on the Internet's potential, see Benjamin R. Barber, *A Place For Us: How to Make Society Civil and Democracy Strong* (New York: Hill and Wang, 1998), 9; Lawrence Lessig, "The Zones of Cyberspace," 48 *Stanford Law Review* 1403, 1407 (1996).
52. *Ashcroft v. ACLU*, 535 U.S. 564, 566 (2002).
53. Ibid., 567.
54. *United States v. American Library Ass'n.,* 539 U.S. 194 (2003).
55. 144 *Congressional Record* § 8611 (1998).
56. Simon, "Cyberporn and Censorship," 1015.
57. *Hearings on the Nature and Threat of Sexual Predators on the Internet Before the House Committee on the Judiciary*, 105th Cong. 1, 3 (Nov. 7, 1997) (statement of Cathy Cleaver, Director of Legal Policy, Family Research Council).
58. Ibid., 1.
59. Elizabeth M. Shea, "The Children's Internet Protection Act of 1999: Is Internet Filtering Software the Answer?" 24 *Seton Hall Legislative Journal* 167, 184 (1999).
60. Ibid., 179.
61. Ibid.
62. *H. R. Rep. No.* 105-775, 19 (1998).
63. *Reno v. American Civil Liberties Union*, 521 U.S. 844, 854 (1997).
64. *United States v. American Library Ass'n.*, 539 U.S. 194 (2003).
65. Critics view anonymity as a threat to accountability and civility on the Internet. Anne Wells Branscomb, "Anonymity, Autonomy and Accountability: Challenges to the First Amendment in Cyberspaces," 104 *Yale Law Journal* 1639, 1660 (1995).
66. Steven Botein, "Printers and the American Revolution," in *The Press and the American Revolution*, Bernard Bailyn and John Hensch, eds. (Worchester, MA; American Antiquarian Society, 1980), 21, 32, 37-40.

67. *Close v. Lederle,* 424 F.2d 988, 990 (1st. Cir. 1970).
68. *Piarowski v. Illinois Community College Dist,* 759 F.2d 625, 632 (7th Cir. 1985).
69. *Claudio v. United States,* 836 F.Supp. 1230, 1235 (E.D.N.C. 1993).
70. 466 U.S. 789 (1984).
71. *Robinson v. Jacksonville Shipyards,* 760 F.Supp. 1486 (M.D. Fla. 1991).
72. Sharon Madere, "Paparazzi Legislation: Policy Arguments and Legal Analysis in Support of Their Constitutionality," 46 *U.C.L.A. Law Review* 1633, 1643 (1999).
73. *Kramer v. Downey,* 680 S.W.2d 524, 525 (Tex. Ct. App. 1984).
74. *Dietemann v. Time, Inc.,* 284 F. Supp. 925, 929 (C.D. Cal. 1968).
75. *Griswold v. Connecticut,* 381 U.S. 479 (1965).
76. *Roe v. Wade,* 410 U.S. 113 (1973).
77. *Lawrence v. Texas,* 539 U.S. 558 (2003).
78. P. G. Ingram, *Censorship and Free Speech: Some Philosophical Bearings* (Burlington, VT: Ashgate Publishing Company, 2000), 109.
79. William N. Eskridge, Jr., "Some Effects of Identity-Based Social Movements on Constitutional Law in the Twentieth Century," 100 *Michigan Law Review* 2062, 2243 (2002).
80. Brief for Appellants at 62-65, *Griswold* (1964 Term, No. 496).
81. *Hill v. Colorado,* 530 U.S. 703 (2000).
82. Ibid., 723, 726.
83. Ibid., 715.
84. Ibid., 715-6.
85. Ibid., 718.
86. Ibid.
87. Ibid., 751.
88. Ibid., 756.
89. Ibid., 756-7.
90. Ibid., 757.
91. Ibid.
92. *Erznoznik v. City of Jacksonville,* 422 U.S. 205 (1975).
93. Leslie Gielow Jacobs, "Is There an Obligation to Listen?" 32 *Univ. of Michigan Journal of Law Reform* 489, 518-19 (1999).
94. Steven Heyman, "Ideological Conflict and the First Amendment," 78 *Chicago-Kent Law Review* 531, 604 (2003).
95. Ibid., 605.
96. *New York v. Ferber,* 485 U.S. 747, 757 (1982); *Ginsberg v. New York,* 390 U.S. 629, 642 (1968) (upholding requirements that restricted the distribution even of printed matter to children).
97. *Butler v. Michigan,* 352 U.S. 380, 383 (1957) (opining that the limits on child protection restrictions have always been that they must not reduce adults to reading "only what is fit for children").
98. *Ginsberg v. New York,* 390 U.S. 629 (1968); *Casey v. Planned Parenthood of Southeastern Pennsylvania,* 510 U.S. 1309 (1994); *South Dakota v. Dole,* 483 U.S. 203 (1987); *State v. Trudell,* 90 Wash. App. 1042, 1998 WL 213517 (Wash. App. 1998).
99. *Bellotti v. Baird,* 443 U.S. 622, 634 (1979).
100. *Pacifica,* 438 U.S. 726, 749-50 (1978).
101. *Pierce v. Society of Sisters,* 268 U.S. 510, 535 (1925); *Wisconsin v. Yoder,* 406 U.S. 205, 232 (1972).
102. Catherine J. Ross, "Anything Goes: Examining the State's Interest in Protecting Children From Controversial Speech," 53 *Vanderbilt Law Review* 427, 434 (2000).

103. *Prince v. Massachusetts*, 321 U.S. 158, 168 (1944).
104. Stanley Ingber, "Rediscovering the Communal Worth of Individual Rights," 69 *Texas Law Review* 1, 73 (1990).
105. Heyman, "Ideological Conflict," 609.
106. *Bethel School District No. 408 v. Fraser,* 478 U.S. 675 (1986).
107. Ibid.
108. *Ginsberg v. State of N.Y.,* 390 U.S. 629 (1968).
109. Ibid., 641.
110. Ibid., 641-42.
111. *Action for Children's Television v. FCC*, 58 F.3d 654, 661-62 (D.C. Cir. 1995).
112. *American Civil Liberties Union v. Reno*, 31 F. Supp. 2d 473, 498 (1999).
113. *Telecommunications Act of 1996*, Pub. L. No. 104-104, 110 Stat. 140.
114. Heyman, "Ideological Conflict," 608.
115. 47 U.S.C. §223(a) and (d) (1996).
116. *Reno v. American Civil Liberties Union*, 521 U.S. 844, 874-85 (1997).
117. 47 U.S.C. §231 (1994 ed., Supp. V).
118. 47 U.S.C. § 231(a)(1).
119. 535 U.S. at 586.
120. 18 U.S. C. § 256(8)(A)-(D).
121. *Ashcroft v. Free Speech Coalition,* 535 U.S. 234 (2002).
122. *Reno*, 521 U.S. 844, 869 (1997).
123. *Butler v. Michigan*, 352 U.S. 380, 383 (1957).
124. *Denver Area Educational Telecommunications v. F.C.C.*, 518 U.S. 727, 755-56; *AIDS Action Comm., Inc. v. Massachusetts Bay Transp. Auth.*, 849 F.Supp. 79, 84 (D. Mass. 1993) (holding that the goal of shielding children from advertisements that used sexual innuendos in promoting condom use was not sufficiently compelling to justify the rejection of those advertisements in public transit spaces).
125. *Bering v. SHARE*, 721 P.2d 918, 921 (Wash. 1986).
126. *Action for Children's Television v. F.C.C.,* 58 F.3d 654, 663 (C.A.D.C. 1995).

5

Implementing a Private Right to Censor

The Legislative Initiative

Determining the Speech Subject to a Private Right to Censor

A private right to censor cannot be implemented through judicial decree. For the same reason that the courts have not crafted a constitutional right to know, they likewise cannot independently implement a right to reject. To do otherwise would be to impose too much uncertainty and subjectivity into the area of First Amendment protections. Consequently, it is up to the legislative branch to enact any measures facilitating or defining a private right to censor; the judiciary's function is limited to one of reviewing those measures under the standards set forth below.

First Amendment doctrine generally denies legislatures any role in shaping or addressing free speech issues. But this rigid refusal to allow any legislative involvement ignores the "changed circumstances" of American media society. The media makes up a significant part of the American economy, not to mention American culture. For the First Amendment to effectively immunize the media from any legislative action regarding the content of its products is to deny democratic control of one of society's largest industries. As one legal scholar observes, the "exclusive concentration on the judicial process for the enhancement of first-amendment values may be the most significant mistake of modern constitutional development."[1]

The first step in implementing a private right to censor is to determine, through a legislative fact-finding process, the particular types of speech or media content that are subject to such a right. Factual inquiries and conclusions must be made regarding the prevalence of offensive, unwanted speech, as well as the public's desire to avoid or reject such speech. A similar type of legislative fact-finding was recognized and supported by the Court in *Turner Broadcasting:* After determining that Congress had engaged in extensive fact-finding regarding the effects of certain rules contained in the Cable Act, the Court deferred to the congressional remedies identified by that fact-finding process.[2]

One focus of legislative inquiry preceding any private-right-to-censor regulations might well encompass an examination of the social harms caused by certain types of entertainment products. Countless studies, for instance, have researched the relationship between violence on television and violent behavior in society. From the earliest days of television, social scientists have been wary of the effects of televised violence.[3] In the 1960s, Senate committees investigated the connection between television violence and rising crime rates.[4] In a six-volume study published in 1972, the U.S. Surgeon General reported the "preliminary indication of a causal relationship" between televised violence and violent behavior.[5] Partly in response to these studies, and partly in response to the growing objections over indecent television programming, the broadcast networks in the 1970s succumbed to FCC pressure and adopted a "family viewing policy," requiring programs broadcast during the first hour of prime time to be suitable for the entire family.[6] But as this policy steadily eroded, Congress eventually reentered the fray and in the early 1990s reconvened hearings on televised violence.

During the hearings preceding the 1996 Telecommunications Act, overwhelming evidence was introduced indicating that children exposed to televised violence are more likely to behave violently than children not so exposed.[7] Among social psychologists, there is a "strong consensus that televised violence causes aggressive behavior."[8] Thus, given these findings, Congress could rationally come to the conclusion that the public should be able to reject certain types of television violence. Congress could also reasonably conclude that in a society as pervasively violent as America, the right of individuals to reject media violence serves a compelling social interest.[9] But this interest could only be acted upon if legislatures are given some flexibility to deal with the rapidly changing entertainment industry and all the ripples it sends throughout society.

Once the particular speech that is to be subject to a private right to censor is identified, the next legislative step is to determine whether that speech is so pervasive that it cannot be easily avoided without some government assistance. Take, for instance, the 1960s rock musical *Hair*, which was subjected to various censorship measures because of its nudity and simulated sex.[10] That play would not be subject to a private right to censor because a theatrical production is easily avoided by unwilling viewers. On the other hand, a private right to censor would justify the V-chip provisions of the 1996 Telecommunications Law, since violent and indecent television programming is not so easily avoided.

As suggested by the Supreme Court in *National Endowment for the Arts v. Finley*,[11] which upheld a law requiring the NEA to consider decency standards when awarding public grants to artists, the government should have the power to help citizens avoid unwanted indecent and offensive speech. The government, though precluded from acting as an independent censor, should be able to serve as a facilitator of a genuinely free communicative process, of which listening and viewing is an essential ingredient.

Facilitating Choice in the Communicative Process

Given the constantly changing ways of delivering entertainment programming that continually challenge the boundaries of social tolerance, legislatures should have the ability to determine what tools are necessary to empower an individual's right to censor unwanted speech. Legislatures should be just as free to facilitate the power to privately censor as they are to facilitate the power to speak. It is not simply the freedom to talk loudly and domineeringly that defines the free speech clause; it is a broader freedom to control one's involvement in the communicative process, whatever form that involvement takes. But to achieve this balancing of speaker and listener freedoms in an increasingly complex social communications process, democratic legislatures must be able to react to the ability of new technologies to expose people to offensive images.

In passing laws aimed at assisting listeners to censor unwanted speech, the legislatures must not overreach. They must go no further than necessary to implement an effective private right to censor. Two requirements must be met regarding any such regulations: First, they must in fact enhance the choice freedoms of the listener; and second, any burdens placed on the speaker (regarding non-political speech) must be balanced by gains to the listener. Because true communicative freedom encompasses a balancing of the rights of speakers and listeners, censorship should not be seen from the single focus of what speech it may be silencing, but from a more balanced focus that includes the increased individual freedom to avoid unwanted, offensive speech.

The First Amendment commands that no burdens on communicative freedoms be placed by the government acting independently, and that no governmental action can result in a *net loss* of communicative freedoms. Since speaking and listening are both integral functions of the process of communication, the government may act to assist one of those functions, particularly if that function is being overwhelmed and subsumed by the other. But the government must never increase the disparity between speaker and listener freedoms; it can only act to lessen that disparity and achieve more of a balance.

As propounded by the natural rights doctrine of the eighteenth century, the freedom to speak is not absolute. Although it is privileged, in the sense that it cannot be banned completely nor abridged even partially for mere governmental desire or convenience, it must be balanced by other equally strong individual rights, such as the right of the listener to be free of intrusive speech and images. However, a burden on speakers can only be justified if necessary to produce an enhancement of listener rights.

It is well established that speech can be regulated when conflicting rights are implicated.[12] For instance, the Court has upheld speech regulations in the vicinity of schools, on the grounds that the learning environment should not be disturbed, and in the vicinity of polling places, on the grounds that the voting process should remain free of any appearance of coercion.[13] In *Austin v. Michigan Chamber of Commerce*, the Court upheld a state law that prohibited corporations from contributing to candidates for state offices.[14] This law obviously burdened the First Amendment rights of those corporations, yet was supported by the compelling state interest in preventing corruption or the appearance of corruption in state elections. But if the government has a compelling interest in toning back the voices of corporations, finding them to be disproportionate to the public support for the view conveyed, then the government should have an interest in letting individuals tone back the media voices that constantly intrude into their lives.

In a case upholding restrictions on unsolicited fax advertisements, the Ninth Circuit held that the government has a substantial interest in preventing the unwanted shift of advertising costs from sender to recipient.[15] Such costs included paper and toner expenses, as well as an interference with the receipt of desired faxes. The court's refusal to make recipients bear the full burden of unwanted speech, however, can be extended beyond the economic realm and into the private-right-to-censor sphere. Moreover, just because a speaker no longer enjoys a completely unburdened right to speak does not mean that her First Amendment liberties have been erased, particularly when those new burdens are necessary to give the recipients a greater level of freedom.

Opt-in communication schemes, which require listeners to take some affirmative action to access certain kinds of speech, impose no greater constitutional costs than do opt-out schemes, which require that unwilling listeners assume all the burdens of avoiding speech. The First Amendment does not mandate that speakers incur absolutely no burdens in exposing listeners to their speech, just as it does not mandate that listeners be virtually powerless to determine the images and speech to which they are exposed. And just as the First Amendment recognizes a right to "non-religion," so too should it recognize a right to "non-speech." As it stands now, however, the marketplace model completely favors the speaker and the willing listener, who is required to make no effort to receive.

Some critics, unhappy with the output produced by the modern media, advocate sweeping regulatory reforms aimed at changing the content of that output. They favor governmental intervention to transform the media marketplace into more of an eighteenth-century public forum dedicated to democratic dialogue.[16] They envision the First Amendment as a positive liberty, enabling individuals to use the courts as a tool in bringing changes to the type of speech prevailing in the public domain. But this notion of positive liberty is just as speaker-focused as the marketplace model; the only difference is that the former focuses on the left-out speakers, rather than on the actual speakers. Under a private-right-to-censor theory, however, the First Amendment is seen as protecting a negative liberty—the individual's independence from control "by external forces or stimuli."[17] Freedom in a negative liberty sense means "immunity from interference."[18] To a listener, this means freedom from being subjected to unwanted speech.

The Judicial Role

Preventing a Ban on Speech by Insuring Alternative Avenues

Under a private-right-to-censor theory, the courts should give deference to legislative accommodations of the public's desire to avoid certain media speech to which it is being exposed. As is their duty regarding any constitutional challenge to legislative actions, courts must ensure that those actions have a rational basis and that the legislatures have fulfilled their fact-finding missions. The courts must ensure that any burdens placed on speakers are balanced by enhancements given to listener rights, and that no net decrease has occurred regarding communicative freedoms. In particular, the courts must ensure that any legislative measure serving a private right to censor not amount to a complete prohibition on the subject speech. Such a ban can be avoided if that speech remains accessible through alternative avenues or formats.

In modern society, speech portraying sex, violence, and vulgarity is in great supply. Not only is it in abundant supply, but it is accessible to the point of being unavoidable. As Justice Powell noted nearly three decades ago in his *Pacifica* concurrence: "I doubt whether today's decision will prevent any adult who wishes to receive Carlin's message in Carlin's own words from doing so."[19] Indeed, as the *Pacifica* Court observed, if an adult wanted to hear vulgarity-laced humor, they could do so in any number of ways—for example, through tapes, records, nightclubs, and late-night broadcasts.

Pacifica suggests that restrictions on indecent speech should be viewed in light of the total supply or expression of that speech through the entire media, not just through the one medium being subjected to restriction. For instance, if sexually graphic songs are restricted from broadcast radio, they will still be available on CDs, music videos, special television channels, and at concerts. There has been no ban on such songs, just a re-channeling of them in a way that facilitates the rights of unwilling listeners. Likewise, a family hour requirement regarding television programming would still leave open a host of other entertainment options for adults, who "have so many alternative ways of satisfying their tastes at other times."[20] Because of the proliferation of so many different communications mediums, censorship should be viewed in terms of the whole spectrum of media. Consequently, a restriction of speech in one medium may be permissible if that speech remains accessible through other mediums.

Prior to the explosion of communications technologies, the censorship of a particular medium (or of a particular way of conveying an idea or information) amounted more or less to a complete censorship of that idea or information. But now, that is not the case. Therefore, when addressing the restrictions placed on a particular kind of output or imagery of one medium, courts should look to the media as a whole, to see if that one restriction is really an unconstitutional infringement on speech. In a media society bulging with unlimited media content, courts should approach censorship issues as they do issues of statutory construction or interpretation: They should look at the whole scheme. They should examine whether the one particular restriction amounts to an effective censorship, in the society at large, of an idea or piece of information. Courts have long distinguished between laws that suppress ideas and laws that only suppress particular expressions of those ideas.[21]

When the First Amendment was ratified, there was essentially one medium for speech. Thus, it can be argued that a speaker only has a right to have his or her speech accessible in some medium(s), but not every medium. To be free, speech does not have to be completely uninhibited in all venues or forums.

Courts have implicitly approved this approach by upholding statutes that restrict speech in one venue while leaving open alternative channels of communications.[22] In *Capital Broadcasting Company v. Mitchell*, the court held that a statute restricting advertising in certain media did not violate the First Amendment, since advertising in other media was still available.[23] In *Urofsky v. Gilmore*, where a group of university professors challenged the constitutionality of a statute restricting state employees from accessing sexually explicit material on computers owned by the state, the court noted that the statute did not prohibit all access to such materials, since an employee could always get permission from their agency head to access the material.[24] In *Hill v. Colorado*, the Court sustained a "buffer zone" regulation restricting the speech rights of abortion protestors, finding that the only restricted avenue of communication was face-to-face dialogue and that the regulation left open ample alternative channels of communication. Similarly, in *Schenck v. Pro-Choice Network*, the Court noted that although speakers had to keep a distance from their intended audience, they remained "free to espouse their message" in various ways from that greater distance.[25] Through its opinions in cases like *Hill* and *Schenck*, the Court seems to be saying that what is important is that the potential of communicative interchange be preserved between speakers and willing listeners. Thus, speech restrictions are valid if willing listeners can still seek out and obtain the speech through an alternative channel.

In addition to ensuring that any private-right-to-censor regulations not amount to a complete ban on the subject speech, the courts must also make certain that the particular medium to which the regulations do apply meets a five-part test. The medium must attract children to its audience. There must be a reasonable chance that the children will be exposed to the unwanted speech. The unwanted speech must be of a type that parents have a legitimate interest in avoiding. The avoidance of such speech must be difficult to achieve without the aid of private-right-to-censor regulations. And the unwanted speech cannot constitute political speech, as described further in chapter 6. Furthermore, if subsequent to the enactment of a private-right-to-censor regulation certain filtering technologies become available that give individuals an effective ability to censor unwanted speech without the aid of that regulation, then the courts at that time should nullify the regulation, since it would be overly restrictive on speech rights without producing a corresponding benefit to listener rights.

The Level of Scrutiny Applied to Private-Right-to-Censor Regulations

Currently, government regulations based on the content of speech receive strict scrutiny, which often results in an almost automatic finding of unconstitutionality.[26] This highest level of scrutiny stems from the marketplace model, being exclusively speaker-focused and seeking to maximize the volume of speech in the public domain. The use of strict scrutiny also stems from a one-sided view of the First Amendment, which ignores listener rights. A more comprehensive view of the First Amendment—one that encompasses the full range of communicative freedoms, involving both speaker and listener—requires a lower level of scrutiny that is not singularly focused on the speaker.

Since private-right-to-censor regulations seek to serve and protect listener rights, they should be judged under a scrutiny that is more balanced toward speaker and recipient. Such a balancing is present in the scrutiny currently given to content-neutral regulations, which are analogous to private-right-to-censor regulations insofar as the government is not acting independently to effectuate a total ban on certain speech, but is simply trying to give individuals greater power to control their own communicative environments.

In *Ward v. Rock Against Racism*, the Court held that a content-neutral speech regulation is permissible so long as it is narrowly tailored to serve a significant governmental interest and so long as alternative channels of communication remain open.[27] This test reflects an intermediate level of scrutiny, known as the *Ward/O'Brien* balancing test.[28] Such a balancing test is also appropriate for private-right-to-censor regulations, since the goal of those regulations is to balance speaker and listener rights. Moreover, an intermediate scrutiny is consistent with the *Pacifica* holding, which states that in the face of a pervasive media that broadcasts indecent material accessible by children, government should be allowed to assist listeners in avoiding such material.

The "floating bubble" law at issue in *Hill v. Colorado* was also evaluated under the lower level of scrutiny used for content-neutral laws. Employing a balancing test, the Court found that the regulations in *Hill* were narrowly tailored to serve significant state interests in protecting listeners from unwanted speech.[29] The Court further found that the regulations did not ban speech altogether, but only regulated the places where it could occur.[30] Based on these findings, the Court approved the floating bubble law, which enabled clinic patients to avoid the speech of abortion protestors.

Examples of Private-Right-To-Censor Regulations

Ideally, technology can make possible a private right of censorship that requires no governmental assistance or intervention.[31] Ideally, a person could pick and choose not only what television stations or channels she wishes to receive, but even the content of particular programs on those channels. As Professors Berman and Weitzner envision:

> In the future, users, instead of the government or network operators, could exercise control with such filtering technology over the information content that they receive in an interactive network environment. User control could be exercised in two ways. First, users could screen out all messages or programs based on information in the header. If a parent wanted to prevent a child from seeing a particular movie or from participating in a particular online discussion group, then the computer or other information appliance used by the child could be set by the parent to screen out the objectionable content. Such features could be protected with passwords assigned, for example, by the responsible adults in the house. Second, the same header information and filtering systems could be used to enable blocking of content based on third-party rating systems. For example, those parents who accept *TV Guide*'s judgment about the presence of nudity and/or violence in particular programs could program their interactive TV sets to screen out all programs that *TV Guide* has classified as violent. Because of the flexibility of

interactive technology, however, we need not rely on just one rating system.... The Christian Coalition or People for the American Way could set up rating systems that would be available on the network to those who desire them. Rather than relying on the judgment of the government, or of the TV network, viewers could limit access to content based on the judgment of a group whose values they share.[32]

If such technology existed, and if Congress mandated that broadcast and direct satellite carriers provide it, then the constitutionality of such a mandate would depend on whether it served a private right to censor under the requirements stated above.

But what if, in the meantime, the technology does not exist to give individuals complete power in their choice of programs they wish to exclude from their home? What if individuals cannot make such decisions without some assistance from government? If in a media society private censorship is seen as the speech of those who are not part of the media stream, and if in a culture deluged with speech a right to filter incoming speech is seen as equivalent with a right to add to that deluge of speech, then the courts must give some power to that right. If there is to be a private right of censor, it must be an effective right. And it must recognize that in the past the television industry has not been very accommodating to efforts at facilitating viewer control. When, at the prompting of the FCC, the networks in the 1970s developed a set of programming guidelines to limit children's exposure to sexually oriented or violent material, a group of television writers and production companies challenged those guidelines, which were then declared unconstitutional because they had been promulgated pursuant to FCC pressure.[33] Furthermore, when representatives of the television industry devised the ratings system to be used in connection with the V-chip, they excluded parental and religious groups from the deliberations.[34]

A private right to censor strives to empower those who have been marginalized by the media culture. Consider, for example, the plight of a conservative religious family. A common charge made against the religiously devout is that they are "out of touch," cut off from the realities of modern culture. And yet, are they to be further cut off just because they do not wish to have television shows like "The Howard Stern Show" or "The Victoria's Secret Fashion Show" or "X-treme Dating" come into their home? Must they completely disconnect the television and be in the minority of those who do not subscribe to cable, just because they don't want to be exposed to what they consider filth? Must they do without CNN and the Discovery Channel and MSNBC just because they don't want their children tuning into sexual "reality" programs?

Perhaps that religious family would subscribe to cable television if they had an effective means of filtering out all the offensive material. If the cable provider was required to carry program ratings from an outside group whose judgment the religious family trusted, perhaps they would feel more comfortable opening themselves to the flood of television programming. Or if the cable provider was made to segregate categories of programming on certain blocks of channels, perhaps the family would feel more at ease surfing through the selections. Would such measures constitute a burden to the cable company? Absolutely. Would they serve the right of people to exclude unwanted programming from their home? Perhaps. The answer would be up to Congress and the courts to provide—to make sure that such measures did in fact serve a right to censor, and that the burdens inflicted on speech did not pose an absolute bar to that speech.

In terms of legislative facilitations of a private right to censor, perhaps nothing could help filter out unwanted media programming better than a truly meaningful and effective ratings system. Currently, nearly all media entertainment carries some kind of ratings system. But as previously noted, these ratings are too generalized to provide any real insight into the nature of the programming. Moreover, since the ratings systems are operated by the media itself, there are significant problems in enforcement. The most frequently mentioned alternatives to the current system are to either have government step in and do the rating, or have Congress force the media companies to rate themselves with a more detailed and enforceable rating system.[35] Both of these, however, are plagued with problems. First, they inject government too intrusively into the regulation of content. Second, they create bureaucratic structures and conflicts that will have little benefit to individuals simply trying to oversee what their children watch. And third, they are not the best way of assisting a private right to censor, nor are they the least restrictive on speech rights.

A better system would be to give private third parties the ability to provide ratings that could in turn be accessible to media users. These outside ratings, done by groups known and trusted by individuals, would inspire a greater confidence and reliance than is accorded to the existing rating system. Clearly, a religious parent would probably trust ratings promulgated by a known religious group more than any ratings imposed by some government bureaucrat or Hollywood employee. Likewise, a feminist parent would probably trust the ratings given by a feminist organization, and a political liberal would probably trust ratings issued by a like-minded organization. If Congress, for instance, mandated that cable operators carry program ratings provided by outside rating groups, such a mandate would serve a private right to censor by giving individuals a better chance to make informed decisions about what programs not to view. The only burden on television programmers, movie studios, and music producers would be to carry these ratings and include them in all advertisements for the particular media product; but because of the support these ratings would provide to viewer and listener rights, any burdens on the media would be more than offset. In fact, the real reason the media would not want to carry such ratings is precisely because it would help educate parents and make them less susceptible to media manipulation.

A legal requirement that media companies carry whatever ratings are provided by outside parties will qualify as content-neutral, since that requirement has no connection to any content distinction made by the government. It is simply akin to a basic labeling or disclosure requirement. Such requirements are constitutional because they serve an informational function, much like warning labels on cigarettes and nutritional labels on packaged foods. In *Meese v. Keene*, the Court held that requiring certain films to be labeled as "propaganda" advances First Amendment interests by mandating disclosure of information to potential viewers.[36] The Court found that this measure would help educate potential viewers as to the nature of the film's content. This same rationale, as also expressed in *Virginia State Board of Pharmacy v. Virginia Citizens Consumer Council*,[37] applies to the disclosure of information regarding whether a television program includes violent or indecent material.

The constitutionality of the content-neutral must-carry rules in *Turner Broadcasting System, Inc. v. F.C.C.*[38] gives strong support for the constitutionality of a "must-rate" system enacted under a private right to censor and that would require television networks or channels to carry program ratings compiled by outside private groups.[39] Professor Wagner argues that a rating scheme could be enacted that would "look quite similar on its face to the content-neutral provisions given intermediate scrutiny in *Turner Broadcasting*."[40] The most common arguments against ratings schemes are that either the government would impose them, or speakers would be forced to rate themselves.[41] But under the proposal made here, neither objection would apply, since it would be outside, private groups doing the rating.

Another example of a private-right-to-censor facilitation would be a requirement that video rental and sales outlets display their products according to ratings. This would help parents entering such an establishment know where to steer their young children, and from where to keep them. Motion picture cineplexes could be required to have a ticket-taker present at the entrance to each individual theater, thereby precluding young children from buying a ticket to a PG-rated film and then, once inside the cineplex, walk into an R-rated film.

Internet providers could be required to offer free of charge a filtering program that parents could use to prevent children from accessing pornographic websites. Perhaps a requirement could also be enacted that precludes new users from even instituting Internet service without first activating or specifically declining a filtering program. Such a requirement would help combat the ignorance that much of the public has regarding filtering devices. It is estimated that only about one-third of American parents with residential Internet service use a commercially available filtering program, despite surveys showing that an overwhelming majority of parents want to restrict their children's access to Internet indecency.[42]

The regulations overturned in *Denver Area* are examples of regulations that would be permissible under a private-right-to-censor theory. At issue in *Denver Area* were requirements that cable operators place indecent programs on a separate, blocked channel, to which a viewer could access only after making a written request.[43] To would-be viewers of such programming, these requirements do not present insurmountable obstacles. Viewers could gain access to the desired programming by simply following the established procedures. Moreover, in terms of relative burdens, it is far easier for adults to access indecent material than it is for parents to have their children avoid it.

The regulations at issue in *Denver Area* are particularly necessary given the failure of current filtering technologies in which the courts seem to be placing so much faith. The Cable Communications Policy Act of 1984, for instance, requires that all cable operators make available by sale or lease a technological device by which the subscriber can block out particular cable channels.[44] But these so-called lock-boxes have proved difficult to obtain and program, and only a negligible number of cable subscribers actually use them.[45] And even though DBS may be easily accessible to children, DBS providers are not required by law to provide blocking devices to subscribers who request them.[46] Consequently, because of the inadequacy of these lock-boxes, the "safe harbor" provisions at issue in *ACT III*, prohibiting indecent broadcast programming between the hours of 6 a.m. and 10 p.m., could well be extended even to the basic, non-premium cable channels.[47]

As a filtering device, the V-chip has also proved disappointing and quite inadequate for the following reasons. First, existing television sets not containing the V-chip may not all be replaced for years, and the chip is only required on larger television sets. Second, nothing can prevent children from watching television at the homes of their friends, whose parents may allow uncontrolled viewing. Third, technologically challenged parents may have difficulty programming the V-chip and hence may shy away from using it entirely; technologically sophisticated children, on the other hand, may be able to crack the system. Safe harbor rules, however, by preventing children from watching indecent programming anywhere and anytime during a good part of the day, would greatly aid the ability of parents to control what media input their children are receiving. Such rules would be consistent with the result in *Crawford v. Lungren*, where the court upheld a statute restricting the ways in which sexually-oriented print material could be distributed, so as to prevent exposure of it to minors.[48] The court found no constitutional violation with a statute banning the sale of "harmful material" from unsupervised sidewalk vending machines.[49]

Consistent with this "safe harbor" approach would be a time-channeling requirement for movie advertisements. For instance, R-rated movies could not be advertised until after a certain hour at night, when the audience viewing those advertisements would most likely be the same audience able to buy a ticket to the film. After all, advertisements for movies have only one purpose: to "entice people to see" that movie.[50]

With the growth of cable and digital, television is far more pervasive than when *Pacifica* was decided. Consequently, the private censorship abilities of the individual are greatly diminished. To combat this loss of viewer rights, the courts should be even more accommodating of legislative efforts to empower viewers and listeners. One such effort might entail regulations requiring an organizational scheme for all cable channels. Such a scheme would place all "news" channels together, all sports channels together, and all educational channels together. Furthermore, these could be placed lower in the channel numbering, with the more adult-oriented stations placed higher. This would help "surfers" avoid stumbling onto unwanted, offensive material. A similar proposal introduced in the U.S. Senate calls for cable companies to offer subscribers a bundle of channels rated according to their content. Subscribers could then either buy channels separately or choose only a family friendly tier of channels.[51]

Private-right-to-censor regulations would also help viewers and listeners exercise some rationality and discipline in their media choices. There is wide agreement among mass media scholars that television programming is not only addictive, but designed to be addictive.[52] There is also wide agreement as to the subliminally manipulative effects of television. Indeed, if it did not have the First Amendment, the television industry, like the tobacco industry, would be swamped with product liability lawsuits.

Perhaps if the burden was shifted more toward opting-in to television versus opting-out, people could make more rational decisions regarding their viewing behavior. Sitting down at the kitchen table, in the middle of the day, studying the schedule of television programming, might lead to a more rational and disciplined decision regarding viewership than plopping down into an easy chair at night, when the mind is tired from a day of work and all too ready to fall into whatever mind-numbing show is being offered on the TV. And perhaps if the V-chip worked in reverse—if people had to affirmatively program into their television the channels and programs they wanted, rather than having to program in the channels and programs they didn't want—individuals could exercise more rationality and judgment in their programming decisions. Contrary to the mindset that television executives want their viewers to have, perhaps by recognizing a private right to censor the courts might help the public break out of the hypnotic trance in which television tries to keep them.

A private right to censor aims to assist those people who "in their capacity as citizens are attempting to implement aspirations that diverge from their consumption choices."[53] Indeed, a fault of the marketplace model is that it can confuse the role of the individual as consumer with that of the individual as citizen.

Resolving the Disparities in First Amendment Doctrines

The Problem with a Medium-Focused Jurisprudence

In its First Amendment doctrines, the Court has focused on the individual medium, creating separate constitutional rules for each medium. The original rationale for this disparity in rules involved the notion of scarcity. Since the broadcast medium operated on a scarce frequency spectrum that could be used by only a certain few broadcasters, the Court gave it the least protective status. And since newspapers were obviously a direct descendent of the media existing at the time of the First Amendment's ratification, and since there was no inherent scarcity limiting the number of newspapers that could exist, that medium was according the highest constitutional protections.

This medium-focused approach, however, is not working in a speech-abundant society. Indeed, there is no longer any such thing as scarcity when it comes to speech, whether the medium be video or print.[54] Nor is their any real difference between broadcast television and cable television, since 80 percent of all households now have both. Nonetheless, rooted in a speaker-focused marketplace model, the courts continue to create First Amendment doctrines based on medium-identity.[55] But because these identities are no longer based on scarcity, the courts are having a difficult time crafting logical rules. For instance, a clear standard of review for content-based regulations of cable programming has still not evolved from the Court's decisions.[56] Consequently, cable television exists "in a doctrinal wasteland in which regulators and cable operators alike could not be sure whether cable was entitled to the substantial First Amendment protections afforded the print media or was subject to the more onerous obligations shouldered by the broadcast media."[57]

The Conflict between the Print and Broadcast Models

In *Turner I*, the Court faced the dilemmas of whether to maintain the disparity in First Amendment treatment of the print and broadcast media, and then whether to apply the print or broadcast model to cable television.[58] The First Amendment status of cable television has been in a sort of legal limbo ever since *City of Los Angeles v. Preferred Communications Inc.*, when the Court stated that cable possessed First Amendment freedoms, but did not specify the exact nature of those freedoms.[59] But even though the Turner Court affirmed that cable programmers are fully protected by the First Amendment, and that the scarcity rationale does not apply to cable, it refused to apply the strict scrutiny used in the print model. Instead, the Court employed an intermediate level of scrutiny that amounted to a halfway compromise between the print and broadcast models.[60]

In *Turner I*, the Court found that the government had made no findings of fact concerning the effects of must-carry on the speech of cable programmers, and thus remanded the case for further findings. On remand, the Court in *Turner II* edged cable even closer to the broadcast model.[61] Indeed, *Turner II* "shows a tolerance for speech-relevant regulatory constraints that is not far from the standard of *Red Lion*, notwithstanding the Court's earlier holding that the *Red Lion* standard was inapplicable to cable."[62] Influencing the Court's decision were the following findings: the market power of cable operators, the fact that most cable systems operate as local monopolies, and the intrusiveness of television and its ability to exploit its audience.[63]

As with so many other cases in which the broadcast and print models clashed, the *Turner* cases tried to piece together a third model to apply to cable television. Though the Court did not want to place the same kind of content restrictions on cable that exist for broadcast, it nonetheless continued to see a difference between the print and television mediums, and between the impact that each medium has on its audience. This confusion and uncertainty over exactly what regulatory standard to adopt for cable also appeared in *Denver Area Educational Telecommunications Consortium, Inc. v. FCC*, where Justice Breyer's plurality opinion retreated from any "rigid single standard" or analogy to any other media. On the other hand, the fact that so many Americans have access to cable threatens the continued maintenance of two different standards, because broadcast channels end up airing increasingly racy programming to financially compete with the cable channels.[64]

In Search of a Unified Model

For decades, free speech advocates have been pushing for all media technologies to have the same constitutional status as does the print medium. In his famous book, *Technologies of Freedom*, Ithiel Poole argued that media convergence and the democratizing aspects of the new media should bring about a convergence of constitutional treatment, and that under the First Amendment all media should be governed by the print model.[65] Poole's argument, as well as the continued arguments of those pushing for uniform application of the print model to all technologies, hinge on a particularly optimistic view of technology.[66]

These advocates point out, correctly it seems, that the new technologies offer opportunities for a dramatically increased array of viewpoints.[67] They argue, again correctly, that the new technologies render obsolete the old scarcity rationale that once justified broadcast regulation. Yet while these advocates focus on likening cable and other technologies to print, in a regulatory and constitutional sense, they ignore the intrinsic differences in those mediums. These differences are summarized by Robert Hughes:

> TV favors a mentality in which certain things no longer matter particularly: skills like the ability to enjoy a complex argument, for instance, or to perceive nuances, or to keep in mind large amounts of significant information, or to remember today what someone said last month, or to consider strong and carefully argued opinions in defiance of what is conventionally called "balance." Its content lurches between violence of action, emotional hyperbole, and blandness of opinion.[68]

What is so often ignored is that the different technologies have different ways of intruding and delivering unwanted speech or images. Consequently, individuals must have different ways in which to censor or reject those images. While so much focus is put on ending the differing constitutional treatment of television and print, for instance, the reality still remains that television is drastically different from print in both content and the way in which that content is delivered. Just a glance at the pages of a newspaper, compared with the daily lineup in a cable schedule, tells everything there is to tell about the contrast between print and television. One focuses primarily on news and information; the other on entertainment. One presents its content in print, requiring a certain level of cognitive deliberation, while the other presents its content in visual images, aimed at eliciting an emotional or instinctive reaction. One concentrates on a logical presentation of views and information, while the other seems increasingly obsessed with pushing ever further the bounds of decency and decorum.

The current demands for greater First Amendment protections for the electronic media are grounded in the same kind of optimistic predictions that were made for cable in the 1970s.[69] Many of the same predictions made today about the Internet were made about cable television. Americans were told to ready themselves for a communications revolution.[70] With all those cable channels, a glorious new content would find a medium: operas, in-depth news programs, book readings. But of course, as Bruce Springsteen's song, "57 Channels and Nothing On," points out, this rosy future has yet to materialize. And as Professor Branscomb argues, if we compare the hype with which cable television was offered to the public in the early 1970s with the current reality, there is much room for cynicism.[71]

In fact, few would now claim that cable has lived up to those rosy predictions, and it is questionable whether the Internet will become the enlightened forum for democratic dialogue that its defenders claim it will. Therefore, given the differences in content between print and electronic media, and given the different ways in which that content is portrayed, it is reasonable to think that courts will continue to treat the various technologies differently. It is also reasonable to expect the courts to continue searching for a third constitutional model that might reconcile the diverging print and broadcast models. Such a model could be one incorporating a private right to censor.

To most viewers, there is no difference between cable and broadcast. They are just channels on a television set. Many viewers do not even know which of the channels are broadcast and which are cable. Consequently, the only standard that should be used to craft constitutional doctrines is not the technological features of the medium, but the ability of viewers to exert control over what content they are exposed to. In a First Amendment sense, viewer and listener freedom is a far more meaningful concept than are abstract notions like spectrum scarcity. As media speech continues to proliferate and become ever more pervasive, First Amendment regulatory models should focus on listener rights, rather than on increasingly obsolete technological distinctions between the different mediums.

Instead of basing First Amendment doctrines on the pervasiveness and intrusiveness of the medium, the courts should look to the pervasiveness and intrusiveness of the content. If the indecent content at issue is itself pervasive, it should not matter whether the medium conveying that content is pervasive. Thus, newspapers could be regulated if they published pornography and if readers had no effective way of acquiring news while at the same time avoiding offensive, unwanted material. As Professor Polivy argues, the Court should analyze speech restrictions according to the degree and type of filtering and exclusion that individuals (readers, viewer, listeners) can perform for the medium in question.[72]

In place of the current hodgepodge of First Amendment doctrines, a private right to censor could provide a simple, unified model for assessing the constitutionality of governmental regulations affecting media speech. This model would keep government out of direct content regulation and would enable the viewer to have greater control. It would eliminate the need for all the false and contrived distinctions that courts must make between indecent, lewd, filthy, vulgar, and obscene programming, because a private right of censorship would give individuals the power to make and effectuate such distinctions. It would also address the ridiculous fallacy promulgated under current First Amendment theory that indecent speech is as vital for a functioning democracy as is political speech.

Notes

1. Stanley Ingber, "Rediscovering the Communal Worth of Individual Rights," 69 *Texas Law Review* 1, 93 (1990).
2. *Turner Broadcasting System, Inc. v. F.C.C.*, 512 U.S. 622, 664-65 (1994).
3. Thomas G. Krattenmaker and Lucas A. Powe, Jr., "Televised Violence: First Amendment Principles and Social Science Theory," 64 *Virginia Law Review* 1123, 1126 (1978).
4. Ibid.
5. Surgeon General's Scientific Advisory Committee on Television and Social Behavior, "Television and Growing Up: The Impact of Televised Violence," 1, 21 (1972).
6. Krattenmaker and Powe, "Televised Violence," 1129; *Writers Guild of America West, Inc. v. F.C.C.*, 423 F. Supp. 1064 (C.D. Cal. 1976) (holding the family viewing hour unconstitutional).
7. *Telecommunications Act of 1996*, §551(a)(4); "The Impact of Interactive Violence on Children: Hearings Before the Senate Comm. on Commerce, Science and Transportation," 106th Cong. (2000) (written testimony of Jeanne B. Funk), reprinted at 2000 WL 11070123, at 4-5.
8. Denise R. Polivy, "Virtue By Machine: A First Amendment Analysis of the V-Chip Provisions of the Telecommunications Act of 1996," 29 *Connecticut Law Review* 1749, 1785 (1997).
9. Ibid., 1786.
10. *Southeastern Promotions, Inc. v. Conrad*, 341 F. Supp. 465 (E.D. Tenn. 1972).
11. *National Endowment for the Arts v. Finley*, 524 U.S. 569 (1998).
12. *Konigsberg v. State Bar of California*, 366 U.S. 36, 50-51 (1961).
13. *Grayned v. Rockford*, 408 U.S. 104 (1972); *Burson v. Freeman*, 504 U.S. 191 (1992).
14. 494 U.S. 652 (1990).
15. *Destination Ventures, Ltd. v. FCC*, 46 F.3d 54 (9th Cir. 1995).
16. G. Edward White, "The First Amendment Comes of Age: The Emergence of Free Speech in Twentieth-Century America," 95 *Michigan Law Review* 299, 376-83 (1996).
17. Steven Heyman, "Righting the Balance: An Inquiry into the Foundations and Limits of Freedom of Expression," 78 *Boston University Law Review* 1275, 1314 (1998).
18. Ibid.

19. *F.C.C. v. Pacifica Foundation*, 438 U.S. 726, 762 (1978) (Powell, J., concurring).
20. Action *for Children's Television v. F.C.C.*, 58 F.3d 654, 667 (D.C. Cir. 1995).
21. *Cohen v. California*, 403 U.S. 15, 19 (1971) (stating that the First Amendment has "never been thought to give absolute protection to every individual to speak whenever or wherever he pleases, or to use any form of address in any circumstances that he chooses").
22. *Frisby v. Schultz*, 487 U.S. 474, 484 (1988); *Moser v. F.C.C.*, 46 F.3d 970 (9th Cir. 1995) (noting that a ban on auto-dialing machines still left abundant alternatives open to advertisers).
23. *Capitol Broadcasting Co. v. Mitchell*, 333 F. Supp. 582, 584 (D.C. 1971)
24. *Urofsky v. Gilmore*, 167 F.3d 191, 194 (4th Cir. 1999).
25. *Schenck v. Pro-Choice Network*, 519 U.S. 357, 385 (1997).
26. *Simon & Schuster, Inc. v. Members of N.Y. State Crime Victims Bd.*, 502 U.S. 105, 124-28 (1991).
27. *Ward v. Rock Against Racism*, 491 U.S. 781, 798, 802 (1989).
28. *United States v. O'Brien*, 391 U.S. 367, 377 (1968).
29. *Hill v. Colorado*, 530 U.S. 703, 725-30 (2000).
30. Ibid., 731.
31. J. M. Balkin, "Media Filters, the V-Chip, and the Foundations of Broadcast Regulation," 45 *Duke Law Journal* 1131, 1143 (1996) (arguing that "perhaps the best [system] would be a pay-per-view system, in which each home could order any available programming at any time of day").
32. Jerry Berman and Daniel Weitzner, "Abundance and User Control: Renewing the Democratic Heart of the First Amendment in the Age of Interactive Media," 104 *Yale Law Journal* 1619, 1633 (1995).
33. *Writers Guild of America v. FCC*, 423 F. Supp. 1064 (C.D. Cal. 1976).
34. Richard Brisbin, "Sex on the Tube," *Focus on Law Studies* (ABA: Fall, 2004), 7.
35. Kevin W. Sounders, "Electronic Indecency: Protecting Children in the Wake of the Cable and Internet Cases," 46 *Drake Law Review* 1, 33 (1997).
36. *Meese v. Keene*, 481 U.S. 465, 481 (1987).
37. *Virginia State Bd. of Pharmacy v. Virginia Citizens Consumer Council, Inc.*, 425 U.S. 748 (1976) (striking down a law banning advertisements of prescription drug prices, on the grounds that consumers would benefit from such disclosures).
38. 512 U.S. 622, 643 (1994).
39. R. Polk Wagner, "Filters and the First Amendment," 83 *Minnesota Law Review* 755, 786-7 (1999).
40. Ibid., 784.
41. Kevin W. Sounders, "Electronic Indecency: Protecting Children in the Wake of the Cable and Internet Cases," 46 *Drake Law Review* 1, 33 (1997).
42. John Schwartz, "It's a Dirty Job; Web Childproofers Keep Surfing Through Muck," *Washington Post*, June 23, 1999, A1.
43. *Denver Area Educational Telecommunications Consortium, Inc. v. F.C.C.*, 518 U.S. 727 (1996).
44. 47 U.S.C. §544(d)(2)(A).
45. *Playboy Entertainment Group v. United States,* 30 F. Supp.2d 702, 712 (D. Del. 1998) (citing survey showing that "less that one-half of one percent" of subscribers have lock-boxes).
46. Joel Timmer, "The Seven Dirty Words You Can Say on Cable and DBS," 10 *Communication Law and Policy* 179, 206 (2005).
47. *Action for Children's Television v. F.C.C.,* 58 F.3d 654 (D.C. Cir 1995).
48. *Crawford v. Lungren*, 96 F.3d 380, 382 (9th Cir. 1996).

49.   Ibid., 385-89.
50.   Joel Timmer, "When a Commercial is Not a Commercial: Advertising of Violent Entertainment and the First Amendment," 7 *Communication Law and Policy* 157, 182 (2002).
51.   James Poniewozik, "The Decency Police," *TIME*, March 28, 2005, 30.
52.   U.S. Sen. Comm. on Commerce, Subcomm. on Communications Impact of Television on Children 3 (1976); U.S. Sen. Comm. on Energy and Commerce, Subcomm. on Telecomm. Social/Behavioral Effects of Violence on Television 11 (1981); P. G. Ingram, *Censorship and Free Speech* (Aldershot; Burlington, VT: Ashgate/Dartmouth, 2000), 113.
53.   Cass R. Sunstein, "Free Speech Now," 59 *University of Chicago Law Review* 255, 288 (1992).
54.   Christopher Yoo, "The Rise and Demise of the Technology-Specific Approach to the First Amendment," 91 *Georgetown Law Journal* 245, 253 (2003) (stating that "the arrival of a wide range of new television technologies promises to render the scarcity doctrine an empirical nullity").
55.   In *Reno v. A.C.L.U.*, the Court focused on which medium-model—print or broadcast—to apply to the Internet.
56.   *Turner Broadcasting System v. FCC*, 512 U.S. 622 (1994).
57.   *Denver Area Educational Telecommunications Consortium, Inc,* 518 U.S. 727, 813-14 (1996)
58.   *Turner Broadcasting System*, 512 U.S. 622, 641 (1994) (addressing the disparity in First Amendment treatment as reflected in *Miami Herald publishing Co. v. Tornillo*, 418 U.S. 241 (1974) (conferring the most protective First Amendment status on the print media) and *Red Lion Broadcasting Co. v. FCC*, 395 U.S. 367 (1969) (granting a much less protective status on broadcasters)).
59.   *City of Los Angeles v. Preferred Communications Inc.*, 476 U.S. 488 (1984).
60.   *Turner*, 662.
61.   *Turner Broadcasting System*, 520 U.S. 180 (1997).
62.   Glen O. Robinson, "The Electronic First Amendment: An Essay for the New Age," 47 *Duke Law Journal* 899, 935 (1998).
63.   *Turner Broadcasting System*, 512 U.S. 622, 633 (1994).
64.   Lynn Smith, "FCC Examining Indecency Laws," *L.A. Times*, January 27, 2004, at 3E.
65.   Ithiel de Sola Pool, *Technologies of Freedom* (Cambridge, MA: Harvard University Press, 1983).
66.   Ibid.
67.   Jeffrey Abramson et. al., *The Electronic Commonwealth The Impact of New Media Technologies on Democratic Politics* (New York: BasicBooks Inc., 1988), 46, 57, 121-2 .
68.   Robert Hughes, "Why Watch It, Anyway?" *New York Review of Books*, February 16, 1995, 38.
69.   Sloan Comm'n on Cable Communications, *On The Cable: The Television of Abundance* (1971).
70.   Ibid.
71.   Anne Wells Branscomb, "Anonymity, Autonomy and Accountability: Challenges to the First Amendment in Cyberspaces," 104 *Yale Law Journal* 1639, 1677 (1995).
72.   Denise R. Polivy, "Virtue By Machine," 29 *Connecticut Law Review* 1749, 1791 (1997).

6

Political Speech and the First Amendment

The Constitutional Distinction Between Political
and Non-political Speech

In the First Amendment hierarchy, political speech resides at the top. Its protection was the primary purpose for the free speech clause. Indeed, one of the catalysts of the American Revolution was the British crackdown on the colonists' rights of free speech and political protest.[1] Later, the debates preceding the adoption of the First Amendment revealed a primary desire to safeguard the kind of political debate necessary for the conduct of self-government.

Because of the primacy of political speech within the First Amendment, it cannot be subject to any governmental infringement, even if that infringement is done for the sake of facilitating a private right to censor. As far as the government is concerned, there are no listener rights when it comes to political speech. Speakers are accorded full and exclusive protection. Strict scrutiny is given to any content-based regulations affecting political speech.

The conclusion that political speech lies at the heart of the First Amendment is based on both original intent and constitutional logic. Not only was political debate and opinion vital to the American crusade for independence, but in the late eighteenth century political speech was really the only kind of speech existing in the public domain. The vast majority of newspaper and pamphlet content was devoted to matters of political importance.[2] Thus, it can be argued that when the framers decided to protect the public expression of speech, they obviously intended such speech to be political; because, in essence, that was the only kind of public speech known to eighteenth-century Americans. Even aside from this original intent, however, constitutional logic dictates that the indispensable role of political speech in sustaining self-government provides the only compelling rationale for the free speech clause. As constitutional scholar Francis Canavan notes, the central reason that freedom of speech is guaranteed by the Constitution "is the successful functioning of the democratic political process."[3]

Despite its prominence in modern free speech theory, individual self-actualization or autonomy cannot provide a sound and logical basis for the First Amendment. As argued earlier, not only does the autonomy argument apply to listeners as well as speakers, but it can apply to non-speech activities as much as it can to speech. Individual autonomy and self-fulfillment can result from winning a game or succeeding at a hobby or even enjoying a meal. Self-fulfillment and self-realization are not uniquely characterized by speech; they can be accomplished "through virtually all voluntary conduct, including one's choice of profession, dress, and consumer goods."[4] Furthermore, there is absolutely no evidence that the framers of the First Amendment were at all concerned with self-realization. Nor is it clear that self-realization is even something to be constitutionally desired. To some people, the promotion of self-realization may mean the freedom to take target practice at other people, or the freedom to destroy a public statue, or the freedom to shout epithets at others. Indeed, self-realization may mean "nothing more than a glorification of self-gratification or social irresponsibility."[5]

If individual autonomy is to justify speech protections, if everyone has an equal right to express anything, then speech itself has ceased being something special. When everyone has an equal right to utter anything, then speech "becomes the equivalent of noise, and free speech theory becomes unintelligible."[6] This is what has happened to free speech theory under the marketplace model, which has been used to protect with equal force every different kind of speech. But where everything from shredding a flag to public nudity to yelling profanities to video games played by a six-year-old is equally protected speech, the First Amendment has ceased to possess any coherent rationale or guiding logic.

The identity crisis of the First Amendment today is not the result of any constitutional deficiency or inadequacy of vision on the part of the framers; instead, the crisis is a result of all the cultural concerns that have attached themselves to the free speech clause. The self-realization movement has demanded freedom for whatever expressive conduct individuals wish to make. The crusade for the breakdown of all sexual restraints or behavioral standards has injected into the public domain a type of speech that, prior to the 1960s, had never been there before. It is movements such as these that have tried to break down the longstanding distinction between protected political speech and other types of "private" speech.

Opponents of the political-speech interpretation of the First Amendment argue that it gives insufficient protection to various kinds of "non-political" speech. And yet, whenever these opponents argue against any restrictions on graphically violent television programming or sexually offensive music lyrics, they cite as their justification the need to protect controversial and unpopular political speech. They rarely argue that violent and sexually explicit entertainment should be protected for its own sake. Therefore, why not codify this position into First Amendment doctrine? Why not specifically state that all controversial and unpopular political speech is indeed fully protected by the First Amendment, but that all non-political speech is subject to the reasoned judgment of communities and their elected representatives?

Unquestionably, the task of defining political speech is a daunting one. The temptation is to define it too broadly, so as to leave room for any and all contingencies; but this temptation must be avoided. Political speech is that speech having a reasoned, cognitive connection to some identifiable political issue that has the potential of entering the legislative arena.[7] It is speech capable of being logically debated, and expressed in a form that can lead to some level of rational debate.[8] It is speech whose primary purpose is to contribute to a public debate, not to be bought and sold as an entertainment commodity having little or no connection to the democratic dialogue. It must be an expression of ideas, rather than a mere product like music CDs, bought primarily for their sound or their maker's celebrity persona, sold in display cases and organized not by any kind of political message but by type of music.

Political speech must be communicated "for its expressive content" and for injecting an idea into the marketplace of ideas.[9] Pornography, on the other hand, is communicated neither for its expressive content nor for injecting an argument into the marketplace of ideas; it is merely "a tool for sexually arousing people."[10] Moreover, pornography is private rather than public in nature. Its purpose "is not to contribute to political, social, and cultural debate, but to stimulate or fulfill the sexual desires of individuals."[11]

Music lyrics would most probably not qualify as political speech, since they are clearly intended to entertain rather than contribute to a rationale debate on some public issue. Sunstein, for instance, would not give constitutional protection to words or expressions that are made "in a way that is not plausibly part of social deliberation about an issue."[12] Even if some particular lyrics do mention some political issue, those lyrics would not be "debatable"—they would not contribute to an ongoing process of debate, in which conflicting opinions would enter into a back-and-forth dialogue. Television news and commentary programs would qualify as political speech, but sitcoms and reality shows would not. Furthermore, the mere mention of a political issue would not be enough to convert a television entertainment show into political speech, just as the reading of a line from *The Federalist Papers* would not convert a pornographic video into political speech. If the producers wish to discuss *The Federalist Papers*, then they can do so directly, with primary focus on the content of that collection. They should not be able to simply tack on some political reference and thereby gain constitutional protection for their pornography. As the Supreme Court has stated, "when 'speech' and 'nonspeech' elements are combined in the same course of conduct, a sufficiently important governmental interest in regulating the nonspeech element can justify incidental limitations on First Amendment freedoms."[13]

The speech in any one medium should be severable. It should be judged separately, on its own merit. Just because some image appears in a newspaper does not mean that it should automatically receive the highest constitutional protection. For instance, if a newspaper published graphic ads for pornographic material, those ads would not constitute political speech and hence could be subject to private-right-to-censor regulations. Similarly, a public sign or banner that expresses a political idea but is laced with profanity may be forced to eliminate that profanity so as to gain full constitutional protection as political speech. Since the profanity adds nothing to the political idea, since it is not expressed so as to inform or enter into debate, since it contains no rational or logical element, the speaker by using it has voluntarily removed his message from the constitutional protections given to political speech. As one scholar has noted about *Cohen v. California*, in which the Court gave constitutional protection to the public display of the message "Fuck the Draft," if the word "fuck" were "forcibly expurgated from public debate, discussion would likely not be substantially impoverished."[14]

Previous case law has held that if a particular medium is essential to democratic communication, then any particular message in that medium is constitutionally protected.[15] But this presumes that any communication in that medium will convey information relevant to democratic decision-making. It also assumes that the medium's audience consists of independent rational agents involved in a dialogue about how we should govern ourselves, "rather than dependent and vulnerable persons addressed monologically."[16] This further assumes that the medium itself is capable of facilitating rational, interactive debate.

Political Speech and the Self-Governance Rationale of the First Amendment

Most every First Amendment textbook contains a section discussing the purposes and values of free speech. There is the truth value, the self-fulfillment value, the safety-valve value, and the democratic self-governance value.[17] This latter value is often associated with the writings of Alexander Meiklejohn.[18] According to Meiklejohn, since self-governance is the whole point of the American experiment, freedom of speech must be defined in relation to self-governance and must protect only that speech necessary for democratic self-rule. The First Amendment only has meaning within the context of the self-governing society in which it operates.

Although Meiklejohn advocated an absolute protection of free speech, he limited that protection to political speech. Essentially, Meiklejohn took a Madisonian view of the First Amendment, seeing its protections as existing primarily to serve democratic processes. Meiklejohn's theory distinguished public speech from private speech. It gave First Amendment protection only to that speech that is truly part of the public arena, and not to speech that is pursued merely for private purposes.[19] Meiklejohn declared that the First Amendment covers only speech that bears, "directly or indirectly, upon issues with which voters have to deal—only, therefore, to the consideration of matters of public interest."[20]

Meiklejohn's theory of the free speech clause stems from an apparent paradox: Whereas the First Amendment is phrased in absolute language, few believe that the government should be absolutely barred from imposing any restrictions on any kind of speech or expressive conduct.[21] Therefore, Meiklejohn argued, the "speech" for which the First Amendment extends absolute protection must be some

subset of all speech in general.[22] The only logical subset, he concluded, is political speech, since the whole focus of the Constitution
is self-government and since free speech plays an indispensable role
in that system.[23]

To illustrate the nature of free expression under the First Amendment, Meiklejohn used the analogy of "the traditional American town
meeting."[24] At such a meeting, freedom of expression is essential
not for the sake of the speaker but for the sake of the assembled
listeners, since "the final aim of the meeting is the voting of wise
decisions."[25] Accordingly, restrictions on redundant speech, or on
speech that does not actually express any idea, are permissible. "What
is essential is not that everyone speak, but that everything worth
saying shall be said," Meiklejohn asserted.[26]

Decades ago, Meiklejohn warned of the exploitative nature of the
electronic mass media: That rather than promoting First Amendment
values of collective decision-making, the media can corrupt and
suffocate them. This warning is especially apt today, revealing as it
does the irrelevance and inadequacies of the marketplace model.
The democratic dialogue is not being stunted by government-im-
posed blockages to speech, but by a flood of distracting speech. The
deluge of amusement and entertainment and consumer marketing is
crowding out the kind of political speech that Meiklejohn argued
was necessary for democracy to thrive. Furthermore, the addictive
quality of much television programming steadily intensifies that
crowding-out effect. In comparison with advertising and entertainment, political speech continues to lose share in the public communications process; it continues to be underproduced relative to the
other kinds of speech.[27] Hence, under the marketplace model, the
democratic dialogue function is being increasingly threatened. As
several communications scholars have noted, "discourse is dying in
America, yet everywhere free speech thrives"[28] On average, Americans spend a greater percentage of their spare time (on average,
50.5 hours per week) watching television than engaging in almost
all other activities taken together.[29]

This crowding-out factor can also be seen in the smothering effect that the electronic media and its entertainment glut has had on
reading. A survey released by the National Endowment for the Arts
reveals a dramatic downward trend in book reading among Americans. Not only is reading in decline among all age and ethnic groups,
but the rate of decline is occurring "more rapidly and more perva-

sively than anyone thought possible."[30] As fast as electronic enter-tainment is advancing, readership is declining. But the crowding-out effect can also act in reverse—it can force people to turn away from all kinds of media. For instance, if parents don't have to con-stantly monitor their children's use of the Internet, perhaps they will allow them to explore that vast store of information more freely.

Alexander Meiklejohn recognized that, in a democratic society with a robust media, the roles of consumer and citizen could easily become blurred or even subsumed; and because of the role of ad-vertisers in determining content, what is being provided in the com-munications market is not necessarily the same as what viewers would like to see. A media culture can actually undermine a democratic culture, if the speech of that media culture centers on amusement and consumption, crowding out political or public interest speech. If the First Amendment means anything, it is that speech is not a consumer commodity like blue jeans.

Meiklejohn's instrumentalist view regarding the First Amendment's focus on political speech has been adopted by other free speech scholars,[31] and most recently by Professors Cass Sunstein,[32] John Hart Ely,[33] and Owen Fiss.[34] Judge Robert Bork has argued that the First Amendment should be limited to protecting only explicitly po-litical speech.[35] Freedom for literature, for instance, would depend not on constitutional mandates but upon the "enlightenment of soci-ety and its elected representatives."[36] This view not only makes Meiklejohn's model more focused and specific, but incorporates a greater trust in the legislative process and a more realistic recogni-tion of modern society. First of all, for most authors, the abolition of the First Amendment would have no practical effect on the dissemi-nation of their work. Second, even if a book were taken out of a library in one community, it would probably be available in the next community down the road, and certainly available for purchase through mail order or the Internet. Third, even if a book were banned because of no First Amendment protection, there would be full con-stitutional protection for any protest that arose over that decision. In other words, while the book itself might not constitute political speech covered by the First Amendment, any protest over a book-banning law would certainly be protected speech. The advantage of the Bork approach would be to give communities the ability to deal flexibly with troublesome media like violent video games. According to Judge Bork, the everything-is-protected message of First Amendment jurisprudence has helped to dull society's duty to make judgments about the state of civilized discourse in the public arena. As long as there is freedom of political speech, controls on other kinds of speech can always be protested; but if the government forecloses political argument, the democratic corrective is unavailable.[37]

Although the Supreme Court has repeatedly emphasized the importance of political speech, it has never specifically ruled that to qualify for high levels of constitutional protection the speech at issue must relate to self-government.[38] However, in *Garrison v. Louisiana*, the Court did state that "speech concerning public affairs is more than self-expression; it is the essence of self-government."[39] In *Buckley v. Valeo*, the Court opined that the First Amendment "affords the broadest protection to political expression."[40] Earlier, the Court had indicated that "a major purpose of the First Amendment was to protect the free discussion of governmental affairs."[41] In *Federal Election Comm'n v. National Conservative Political Action Comm.*, the Court described political speech as being "at the core of the First Amendment."[42] Ruling on an action brought by an ex-government employee who claimed she was fired in retaliation for criticisms she made about her employer, the Court focused on whether the speech was political in character and whether it addressed "a matter of public concern," stating that if the speech was not of public concern there was no First Amendment protection.[43] And in *FCC v. League of Women Voters*, the Court ruled that "editorial opinion on matters of public importance...is entitled to the most exacting degree of First Amendment protection," and that the "Framers of the Bill of Rights were most anxious to protect...speech that is indispensable to the discovery and spread of political truth."[44]

Over the decades, a kind of hierarchy of speech has evolved within First Amendment jurisprudence. At the bottom of this hierarchy is speech that receives no constitutional protection. Such speech includes obscenity, defamation, and fighting words.[45] Higher on the ladder is what First Amendment scholars have called "low value" speech, which includes commercial speech.[46] And at the top of the hierarchy is all the speech that qualifies for full First Amendment protection.[47] The most frequently cited speech occupying this top rung is political speech. As the Court has declared, there exists "practically universal agreement that a major purpose of [the First] Amendment [is] to protect the free discussion of governmental affairs."[48] In *FCC v. League of Women Voters*, the Court stated that "expression on public issues has always rested on the highest rung of the hierarchy of First Amendment values."[49]

Generally, indecent speech has fallen in the top category, entitled to full First Amendment protection.[50] Indecent speech is speech that "borders on obscenity,"[51] but may also include "patently offensive" material that nonetheless has some literary or artistic merit.[52] However, in certain contexts, indecency falls to a "low value" speech. In the broadcast media, for instance, indecent speech receives a lower level of protection, as suggested by *Pacifica*'s reference to the "slight social value" of indecent speech.[53] And in approving a school district's sanctioning of a student speech containing sexual innuendo and profane language, the Supreme Court drew a clear distinction between such speech and a more serious message of political protest, which would be protected.[54]

Even though the Court has implicitly recognized a loose form of speech hierarchy, it has stopped short of any formal recognition. Just when the Court seems about to clarify the First Amendment hierarchy and the place of political speech within that hierarchy, it backs away and refuses to make any such distinctions. In *Virginia State Board of Pharmacy v. Virginia Citizens Consumer Council*, for instance, the Court even suggested that commercial speech might be *more* important than political speech: A "consumer's interest in the free flow of commercial information...may be as keen, if not keener by far, than his interest in the day's most urgent political debate."[55] Despite acknowledging that some commercial speech lacks any public interest or importance, the Court refused to distinguish between those types of speech and other speech that did possess a degree of public interest.[56] Nor has the Supreme Court built upon the approach it used in *Connick v. Myers*—that the First Amendment only protected speech that related to "matters of public concern." It has not rested constitutional protection upon a definition of public discourse that distinguishes "speech about matters of public concern from speech about matters of purely private concern."[57]

When Alexander Meiklejohn first articulated his democratic dialogue theory, the danger to free speech lay in governmental restrictions on radical opinion. At the time, Congress was targeting the speech of groups like the Communist Party.[58] But today, the assault on political speech may well be coming from the overabundance of nonpolitical speech. Therefore, the courts need to more clearly define the type of speech that warrants constitutional protection.

The intermingling of the private right to censor with Alexander Meiklejohn's theory of free speech attempts to incorporate what the courts have long recognized: that not all speech is of equal importance or priority under the First Amendment. But unlike Meiklejohn's theory, the private-right-to-censor model does not deny First Amendment protection to non-political speech; it just holds that for some non-political speech the right to censor may be stronger than the right to a burden-free access. Or put another way: Different kinds of speech may have different censorship quotients; and a higher censorship quotient may justify greater burdens of access. Therefore, the test for a private right to censor may very well turn out differently for different kinds of speech. In an age of speech abundance, the First Amendment should not view speech/censorship issues simply as an on-off valve, but as a faucet with varying degrees of "on."

Defining the Distinction

Very few First Amendment scholars would disagree with the assertion that political speech occupies the pinnacle of the First Amendment hierarchy. The problem is not valuing political speech, but in distinguishing political speech from all other kinds of speech. And it is largely because of this problem that critics dismiss a First Amendment model that protects only political speech.

As difficult a task as it is, however, the job of clarifying the parameters and characteristics of the kind of speech protected by the First Amendment is one that needs to be done, especially as the amount of "speech" in our media society increases so rapidly. Meiklejohn knew it was not easy to find a definition for political speech, but the mere difficulty of the task is no reason to abandon it. As Professor Sunstein notes, "there is no way to operate a system of free expression without drawing lines." Not all words or pictures are entitled to full constitutional protection. The question is not "whether to draw lines, but how to draw the right ones."[59]

Anticipating the problems that a marketplace model would bring, Professor Wigmore in 1920 argued that a civilized society had the capacity to distinguish those utterances that enhanced the body politic from those that corroded it. Criticizing Justice Holmes's marketplace metaphor, Wigmore maintained that citizens had both a moral and legal right to repress speech that passed the boundaries of civilized interchange and threatened the fabric of the community.[60] Decades later, the Supreme Court echoed this view when it recognized that certain low value speech plays "no essential part of any exposition of ideas, and [is] of such slight social value as a step to truth that any benefit that may be derived from [it] is clearly outweighed by the social interest in order and morality."[61]

The first defense to the claim that judges cannot possibly make the kind of speech distinctions necessitated by Meiklejohn's theory is to point out that the Supreme Court has stated that absolute precision is not required in constitutional doctrines.[62] Even the most stringent vagueness test does not "expect mathematical certainty from our language."[63] The second defense is that, even though the courts have shied away from attempting any clear differentiation between political and nonpolitical speech, they are well accustomed to making content distinctions in First Amendment case law. Just as courts have had to define concepts as amorphous as religion, so too have they carved out definitions of various kinds of speech categories.

Courts have long distinguished incitement from advocacy,[64] commercial speech from noncommercial speech,[65] and obscenity from indecency.[66] In defamation actions, a court must distinguish between fact and opinion—a distinction that is rarely clear-cut.[67] That court must also, in ruling whether a statement is defamatory, determine the often ambiguous issue of whether that statement has lowered the reputation of the plaintiff "in the eyes of the community."[68] Furthermore, if defamatory speech involves a public figure, the highest of First Amendment protections apply,[69] whereas if the speech addresses a purely private concern, then the defamation law operates with little First Amendment limitations.[70]

The field of copyright law is strewn with content distinctions. Facts and ideas may not be copyrighted, but "creative expression" may be; thus, a distinction must be made between copyrightable expression and uncopyrightable facts and ideas.[71] Copyright law also favors originality over repetition; the "further an author gets from what has gone before, the more protection he will get."[72] In determining copyright status, courts must decide whether a work is "original" or whether it is simply "interpretive" or "viewpoint expressive." Obviously, trying to determine whether a work is sufficiently "original" from everything that has preceded it is fraught with uncertainty and ambiguity, just as is the determination of whether speech is obscene or indecent.[73]

Courts must likewise make content distinctions in cases involving commercial speech. In contrast to political speech, commercial speech occupies a "subordinate position" in the scale of First Amendment values.[74] To assess the degree of protection given to commercial speech, courts must for instance determine whether the speech is false or misleading, or just advertising "puffery."[75]

In a long line of cases involving speech distinctions similar to the political/non-political differentiation, courts have ruled on whether certain speech addresses public matters or mere private concerns. This issue arose in *Diaz v. Oakland Tribune*, a disclosure of private facts tort case.[76] Diaz, the first female student body president at a community college, sued the *Oakland Tribune* after it published the fact that she was a transsexual. In determining whether the case could proceed, the court had to rule on the newsworthiness of this fact, on whether it was a matter of public interest or mere private concern. A similar issue existed in *Briscoe v. Reader's Digest Association*, in which Reader's Digest was held liable for revealing that eleven years earlier Briscoe had been convicted of armed robbery.[77] Even though ruling that the information was newsworthy, the court found that revealing Briscoe's identity eleven years after the crime was not "of legitimate public interest."[78]

Courts have also adopted a public/private speech distinction in cases involving the government's ability as employer to discipline its employees. In *Connick v. Meyers*, the Court held that the government may restrict the speech of its employees if that speech deals with matters of private concern.[79] Likewise, in *Urofsky v. Gilmore*, where a group of state university professors challenged the constitutionality of a law restricting them from accessing sexually explicit material on computers owned by the university, the court stated that the applicability of the First Amendment depended on whether the speech at issue (the sexually explicit material) touched "upon a matter of public concern."[80]

The public/private concern distinction has similarly been employed in libel cases. In *Dun & Bradstreet v. Greenmoss Builders*, for instance, the Court ruled that in libel cases involving false statements on matters of purely private concern, plaintiffs may be awarded punitive and presumed damages without a showing of actual malice.[81]

Courts have also had to make political/non-political speech distinctions when addressing disputes stemming from public art decisions made by the government. In *Piarowski*, involving the government's removal of artwork from a public location, the court ruled that the work in question was not political speech and that the artist "intended no political statement" be made by his work.[82] Concluding that the artwork was "sexually explicit and racially insulting," the court approved its removal.[83] Likewise, in *Close*, the court found that plaintiff's art did not "express political or social thought."[84] And in *Claudio*, the court was adamant in its requirement of an identifiable political message, noting that the artist's conduct suggested "not that he desired to express a viewpoint, but that he sought to vex the government and to generate such self-serving notoriety as might be attendant to this dispute."[85]

Not only are content distinctions possible, but given the rapidly increasing volume and diversity of speech, such distinctions are becoming vital. Without singling out political speech from the vast sea of entertainment speech, the danger is that the former will eventually be swamped by the latter. Political speech will not wither because of government censorship, but simply because it has been crowded-out from the public domain by all the entertainment and marketing speech. Seen from this perspective, private censorship can be viewed not as an oppressor but as a stimulant of speech. By constraining the dominance of low value speech, private censorship may help to energize political speech, in the same way that ridding a garden of weeds will lead to a fuller growth of flowers. It may also help to channel political speech from "undebatable" venues (such as music recordings) into more debatable, informative venues (such as books and magazines).

Distinguishing political from nonpolitical speech, and then giving greater protection to the former, may also help to increase public involvement in the political dialogue. People may participate more in the public communicative process if they do not always have to endure so much offensive speech in the course of gaining access to that process. This is the implied message of cases like *Burson v. Freeman*, where the Court upheld a regulation prohibiting the solicitation of votes within 100 feet of a polling place: that people may be less apt to participate in the political process if they are forced to endure the intrusion of unwanted speech on the way.[86]

An explosion in its growth contradicts the claims that sexually explicit speech is a fragile and vulnerable speech, easily "spooked" by repressive community attitudes, its existence dependant on the highest levels of constitutional protection. For instance, of all the different kinds of academic or social-concerns journals that could be started, students at Harvard University initiated a magazine devoted to "a subject that just doesn't get enough attention: sex."[87] The premiere issue contained erotic fiction, nude photos, and poetry about sex. And just a year earlier, Yale University students organized "Sex Week at Yale." Speakers included a porn star, the creator of "Girls Gone Wild," and a masturbation expert—all undoubtedly of great educational value to students at one of the nation's top universities.

Contrary to the lofty claims of many pro-speech advocates, an unrestrained sexual expression does not necessarily liberate the individual. Instead, the increasingly sexualized character of public discourse may well cause people to be more manipulated by the mass media and by their own over-stimulated instinctual urges. It may cause people to turn away from public involvement and dwell exclusively on the indulgence of their private desires.[88] Indeed, the sexual obsession of modern culture plays "a key role" in heightening individual preoccupation with pleasure and consumption.[89] Aside from a sexualized discourse and sexualized entertainment, sex is being used more frequently to sell all kinds of consumer products.[90] Thus, instead of producing independent-minded individuals, the dominance of sex in the public discourse may simply reinforce certain dehumanizing aspects of mass culture—by transforming people into sexually manipulated robots and by creating a herd-like mentality in which everyone is shackled to the same sexual pursuits.

Some critics also say that the sexualized public discourse promotes a commodification of the body.[91] Others claim that sexually themed speech strips women of their dignity and interferes with the personal and business relationships of women who have to deal with men who watch such speech.[92] Furthermore, mounting evidence also suggests that sexualized images on television can shape teens' attitudes toward sex. Teenaged girls and young women who watched as little as twenty-two hours a month of prime time television are more likely to have more sex partners and to take a more recreational view of sex than those who watched less television.[93]

Prior to the Supreme Court cases that gave pornography full constitutional protection, *Hustler* magazine and the Playboy Channel probably would have been highly restricted. Yet, contrary to the arguments used to defend pornography, it does not appear that the pre-1960s era was a political dark age. Furthermore, "increasing leniency on pornography in the past three decades…does not seem to have corresponded with an increased quality of debate on public issues."[94] This implies that sexually explicit speech "bears little connection to the core values of the First Amendment."[95]

The failure of courts to define political speech and articulate special constitutional protections for that speech is particularly evident in the judicial opinions dealing with the First Amendment status of video games. In those cases, the courts have refused to treat offensive and violent video imagery any different than the most historically acclaimed literary works. Given this trend in how courts are dealing with new media forms like video games, perhaps it is time to revisit Alexander Meiklejohn's theories on the First Amendment and the type of speech it protects.

Notes

1. Patrick M. Garry, *The American Vision of a Free Press* (New York: Garland Publishing, Inc 1990), 46.
2. Ibid, 54.
3. William A. Donohue, *Twilight of Liberty: The Legacy of the ACLU* (New Brunswick, NJ: Transaction Publishers, 1990), 191.
4. Stanley Ingber, "Rediscovering the Communal Worth of Individual Rights: The First Amendment in Institutional Contexts," 69 *Texas Law Review* 1, 19 (1990).
5. Ibid., 20.
6. G. Edward White, "The First Amendment Comes of Age: The Emergence of Free Speech in Twentieth-Century America," 95 *Michigan Law Review* 299, 391 (1996).
7. Cass R. Sunstein, *Democracy and the Problem of Free Speech* (New York: Free Press, 1993), 130 (defining political speech as speech "both intended and received as a contribution to public deliberation about some issue").
8. Robert Bork, *Slouching Towards Gomorroh* (New York: Regan Books, 1996), 148.
9. Eugene Volokh, "Freedom of Speech and Information Privacy: The Troubling Implications of a Right to Stop People from Speaking About You," 52 *Stanford Law Review* 1049, 1099 (2000).
10. Ibid.
11. Steven Heyman, "Ideological Conflict and the First Amendment," 78 *Chicago-Kent Law Review* 531, 605 (2003).
12. Cass R. Sunstein, "Free Speech Now," 59 *University of Chicago Law Review* 255, 312 (1992).
13. *United States v. O'Brien*, 391 U.S. 367, 376 (1968).
14. Volokh, "Freedom of Speech and Information Privacy," 1095.
15. James Weinstein, "Speech Categorization and the Limits of First Amendment Formalism," 54 *Case Western Reserve Law Review* 1091, 1121 (2004).
16. Ibid., 1122.
17. Geoffrey Stone et al., *Constitutional Law*, 2d ed. (Boston: Little, Brown & Co., 1991), 1017-1024.
18. Alexander Meiklejohn, *Free Speech and Its Relation to Self-Government* (New York: Harper, 1948); Alexander Meiklejohn, *Political Freedom: The Constitutional Powers of the People* (New York: Oxford University Press, 1965).

19. Rodney Smolla, *Smolla and Nimmer on Freedom of Speech* (Deerfield, IL: Clark Boardman Callahan, 2003), 2-30.
20. Meiklejohn, *Political Freedom*, 79.
21. Ibid., 19-21.
22. Ibid., 24-28.
23. Ibid., 79-80.
24. Ibid., 24.
25. Ibid., 26
26. Ibid.
27. Ronald K. L. Collins and David M. Skover, *The Death of Discourse* (Boulder, CO: Westview Press, 1996), 7, 213.
28. Ibid., xix.
29. Ibid., 5.
30. Bruce Weber, "Fewer Noses Stuck in Books in America, Survey Finds," *New York Times*, July 8, 2004, B1.
31. Alexander M. Bickel, *The Morality of Consent* (New Haven, CT: Yale University Press, 1975), 62 (declaring that "the First Amendment should protect and indeed encourage speech so long as it serves to make the political process work"); Lillian R. BeVier, "The First Amendment and Political Speech: An Inquiry into the Substance and Limits of Principle," 30 *Stanford Law Review* 299, 358 (1978) (contending that "the sole legitimate First Amendment principle protects only speech that participates in the process of representative democracy"); Harry Kalven, Jr., "The New York Times Case: A Note on the Central Meaning of the First Amendment," 1964 *Supreme Court Review* 191, 208 (1964) (arguing that the First Amendment "has a central meaning—a core of protection of speech without which democracy cannot function").
32. Cass Sunstein, "Free Speech Now," 59 *University of Chicago Law Review* 255, 301-12 (1992) (advocating a "two-tier First Amendment," in which courts would subject restrictions on political speech to the strictest scrutiny, while applying a lower level of scrutiny to "lower value," nonpolitical speech).
33. John Hart Ely, *Democracy and Distrust: A Theory of Judicial Review* (Cambridge, MA: Harvard University Press, 1980).
34. Owen M. Fiss, "Free Speech and Social Structure," 71 *Iowa Law Review* 1405 (1986).
35. Robert Bork, "Neutral Principles and Some First Amendment Problems," 47 *Indiana Law Journal* 1, 20 (1971).
36. Ibid., 28.
37. Sunstein, "Free Speech Now," 306.
38. Smolla, *Smolla and Nimmer,* 2-33.
39. *Garrison v. State of La.*, 379 U.S. 64, 74-75 (1964).
40. 424 U.S. 1, 14 (1976).
41. *Mills v. Alabama*, 384 U.S. 214, 218 (1966).
42. 470 U.S. 480, 493 (1985).
43. *Connick v. Myers*, 461 U.S. 138, 145-46 (1983).
44. *F.C.C. v. League of Women Voters of California,* 468 U.S. 364, 375-6, 383 (1984).
45. *Miller v. California*, 413 U.S. 15, 24 (1973) (holding that obscenity is not protected by the First Amendment).
46. *Dun & Bradstreet v. Greenmoss Builders, Inc.*, 472 U.S. 749, 758 (1985); Eugene Volokh, *The First Amendment: Problems, Cases and Policy Arguments* (New York: Foundation Press, 2001), 114-7 (discussing "low value" speech); *Ohralik v. Ohio State Bar Ass'n*, 436 U.S. 447, 456 (1978) (stating that commercial speech enjoys "a limited measure of protection, commensurate with its subordinate position in the scale of First Amendment values").

47. *Cannabis Action Network v. City of Gainesville*, 231 F.3d 761, 775 (11th Cir. 2000).
48. *Burson v. Freeman*, 504 U.S. 191, 196 (1992).
49. *F.C.C.*, 468 U.S. 364, 381 (1984).
50. *Reno v. American Civil Liberties Union*, 521 U.S. 844, 874 (holding that any government attempt to impose a content-based restriction on indecent speech is strictly scrutinized).
51. *Alliance for Community Media v. F.C.C.*, 56 F.3d 105, 130 (D.C. Cir. 1995).
52. Ibid.,130.
53. *F.C.C. v. Pacifica Foundation*, 438 U.S. 726, 746 (1978).
54. *Bethel School Dist. No. 403 v. Fraser*, 478 U.S. 675, 680 (1986).
55. *Department of Revenue of State of Wash. v. Association of Washington Stevedoring Companies*, 435 U.S. 748, 763 (1976) (emphasis added).
56. *Virginia State Board of Pharmacy v. Virginia Citizens Consumer Council*, 425 U.S. 748, 764-5 (1976) (stating that "no line between publicly interesting or important commercial advertising and the opposite kind could ever be drawn").
57. Robert C. Post, "The Constitutional Concept of Public Discourse: Outrageous Opinion, Democratic Deliberation and Hustler Magazine v. Falwell," 103 *Harvard Law Review* 601, 667 (1990).
58. *American Communications Ass'n v. Douds*, 339 U.S. 382 (1950) for general discussion.
59. Sunstein, "Free Speech Now," 255, 308.
60. John H. Wigmore, "Abrams v. United States: Freedom of Speech and Freedom of Thuggery in War-Time and Peace-Time," 14 *Illinois Law Review* 539, 552-54 (1920).
61. *Chaplinsky v. New Hampshire*, 315 U.S. 568, 572 (1942).
62. *Kolender v. Lawson*, 461 U.S. 352, 361 (1982).
63. *Grayned v. City of Rockford*, 408 U.S. 104, 110 (1972).
64. *Brandenburg v. Ohio*, 395 U.S. 444, 448 (1969).
65. *Bolger v. Youngs Drug Prods. Corp.*, 463 U.S. 60, 64 (1983).
66. *FCC v. Pacifica Foundation*, 438 U.S. 726 (1978).
67. *Milkovich v. Lorain Journal Co.*, 497 U.S. 1, 19 (1990).
68. *Tucker v. Fischbein*, 237 F.3d 275, 283 (3d Cir. 2001).
69. *Curtis Publishing Co. v. Butts*, 388 U.S. 130, 155 (1967).
70. *Dun & Bradstreet, Inc.*, 472 U.S. at 761-63.
71. *Harper & Row v. Nation Enterprises*, 471 U.S. 539, 556, 560 (1985).
72. Rebecca Tushnet, "Copyright as a Model for Free Speech Law," 42 *Boston College Law Review* 1, 49 (2000).
73. *Miller v. California*, 413 U.S. 15 (1973); *F.C.C.*, 438 U.S. 726, 748 (1978).
74. *Unites States v. Edge Broad. Co.*, 509 U.S. 418, 430 (1993).
75. *44 Liquormart v. Rhode Island*, 517 U.S. 484, 504 (1996).
76. *Diaz v. Oakland Tribune*, Inc.188 Cal. Rptr. 762 (Ct. App. 1983).
77. *Briscoe v. Reader's Digest Association*, 483 P.2d 34 (Cal. 1971).
78. Ibid., 43.
79. *Connick*, 461 U.S. 138 (1983).
80. 167 F.3d 191, 194-96 (4th Cir. 1999).
81. *Dun & Bradstreet, Inc.*, 472 U.S. 749 (1985).
82. *Piarowski v. Illinois Community College Dist.*, 759 F.2d 625, 628, 632 (7th Cir. 1985).
83. Ibid., 632.
84. *Close v. Lederle*, 424 F.2d 988, 990 (1st Cir. 1970).

85.   *Claudio v. U.S.*, 836 F. Supp. 1236 (E.D.N.C. 1993).

86.   *Burson v. Freeman*, 504 U.S. 191 (1992).

87.   Barbara Kantrowitz, "Dropping the H Bomb," *Newsweek*, June 7, 2004, p. 45.

88.   Patrick Brantlinger, *Bread and Circuses: Theories of Mass Culture as Social De-cay* (Ithaca, NY: Cornell University Press, 1983), 19, 22.

89.   Lili Levi, "The Hard Case of Broadcast Indecency," 20 *Review of Law & Social Change* 49, 66 (1992-93).

90.   Sylvia Law, "Rethinking Sex and the Constitution," 132 *University of Pennsylvania Law Review* 955, 961 (1984).

91.   Stephen J. Schnably, "Property and Pragmatism," 45 *Stanford Law Review* 347, 391 (1993).

92.   Catherine MacKinnon, *Only Words* (Cambridge, MA: Harvard University Press, 1993).

93.   Cheryl Wetzstein, "TV Teaches College Students Casual Sex is OK, Study Finds," *Washington Times*, September 13, 1999, A8.

94.   John Charles Kunich, "Natural Born Copycat Killers and the Law of Shock Torts," 78 *Washington University Law Quarterly* 1157, 1212 (2000).

95.   Ibid.

7

Defining Speech in an Entertainment Age: The Video Game Example

In *Interactive Digital Software Association v. St. Louis County*, the Eighth Circuit overturned an ordinance that restricted children's access to graphically violent video games.[1] As the court stated, "we are obliged to recognize that [video games] are as much entitled to the protection of free speech as the best of literature."[2]

Recently the courts have reversed direction from their earlier decisions in which video games were not seen as protected speech, and they have made this reversal in a rather cursory manner. The judicial opinions have rested more on mere presumptions than on any real examination of what kind of speech the First Amendment aims to protect. These decisions carry implications far beyond just the entertainment realm of video games, because they set a precedent for how the courts will determine whether new forms of technology constitute protected speech. They set the mold for future cases that must deal with even newer technologies and even more unexpected forms of entertainment. For in the media society America has become, the one sure thing is that there will continue to be new and different technologies of entertainment. Yet if every new technology is automatically given First Amendment status, as seems to be the case with video games, then there is a risk that the First Amendment may become meaningless through an endless process of dilution.[3]

The Concerns Giving Rise to the Video Game Controversy

The statute at issue in *Interactive Digital* was similar to other states' attempts to regulate violent video games. And even after federal courts struck down similar regulations in Washington and Missouri, Governor Rod Blagojevich of Illinois still proposed a law making it a misdemeanor to sell violent and sexually explicit video games to minors.[4] This regulatory trend followed in large part from the belief that such games were a causal factor in various high school shootings that had recently occurred.

In 1997, Michael Carneal opened fire on a prayer group at his school, killing three girls and wounding five people.[5] On March 24, 1998, thirteen-year-old Mitchell Johnson and eleven-year-old Andrew Golden shot and killed four girls and a teacher while they were evacuating school during a fire alarm.[6] Kip Kinkel went on a shooting spree in his school's cafeteria on May 21, 1998, killing two students and wounding twenty-two others.[7] And on April 20, 1999, in the worst school shooting in history, Eric Harris and Dylan Klebold killed twelve students and a teacher at Columbine High School, before themselves committing suicide.[8]

In the aftermath of these shootings, victims and commentators and psychologists alike blamed the graphic violence in video games that the shooters had frequently played. The Columbine shooters, Harris and Klebold, were described as "avid, fanatical and excessive consumers of violent…video games."[9] Consequently, the families of many of the victims filed personal injury lawsuits against the makers of those video games. In their suit against the video game companies, for instance, relatives of the victims of the Columbine shootings alleged that video games had made violence pleasurable to Harris and Klebold and had trained them to shoot and kill.[10] The lawsuits relied on research that characterized violent video games as "firearms trainers" and "murder simulators."[11] Various studies described video games as vehicles for "operant conditioning" (in which players are rewarded for killing) and "stimulus addiction" (whereby players come to crave the emotional response they feel when engaging in virtual violence).[12] Some psychologists even claimed that playing violent video games effectively desensitizes players to killing, and to death in general.[13] As one scholar noted, "compared to other forms of entertainment, video games are disproportionately concerned with violence."[14] In one of the best-selling games of 2004, *Grand Theft Auto: San Andreas*, players control a character called CJ, who beats people until they are lying dead in a pool of blood, steals cars, runs over pedestrians who get in his way, and has sex with prostitutes in his car.[15]

Empirical studies looking at the effects of violent video games on children have asserted that "a preference for violent games is correlated with adjustment problems and negative self-perceptions in some groups of children."[16] The playing of video games has been found to be "positively related to aggressive behavior and delinquency."[17] Several experts suggest that this relation could be similar to the relation between tobacco use and cancer. Just as not every smoker will develop cancer, neither will every video game user behave more violently. But a direct correlation does exist, similar to the connection of tobacco use with cancer, between the playing of violent video games and developing aggressive behavior.[18]

Violent video games, of course, are just one manifestation of a whole media culture of violence. The film *Natural Born Killers*, for instance, has been implicated in more than a dozen real-life murders.[19] On February 2, 1996, a fourteen-year-old devotee of the film, wearing the same clothes as the main character in the film, walked into a classroom and started firing an assault rifle, killing his teacher and several students.[20] Another fourteen-year-old boy, after being accused of decapitating a thirteen-year-old girl, told police that he wanted to be "famous like the natural born killers."[21] A Georgia teenager accused of killing an eighty-two-year-old man shouted at the television cameras, "I'm a natural-born killer."[22] And a teenage boy in Utah, obsessed with the film, shaved his head and bought the same distinctive glasses as the movie's main character, and then killed his stepmother and half sister.[23]

Music lyrics have had similar effects. Two Las Vegas police officers were ambushed and shot by four juveniles who claimed to be acting out a song titled "Cop Killer" by "gangsta" rap artist Ice-T. After their arrest, the juveniles continued to chant the lyrics, which included the chorus: "Die, die, die, pig, die! F–k the police! Die, die, die, pig, die."[24] In Milwaukee, two seventeen-year-olds shot a police officer because, as the shooter told police, the angry lyrics of a rap song had "geeked him up" to stalk and kill the officer.[25]

The majority of studies on the impact of media violence on children find a high correlation between exposure to media violence and violent behavior.[26] Many also report a correlation between exposure to media violence and an increased acceptance of violent behavior in others.[27] A fifteen-year study links children's viewing of violent TV shows to later aggression as young adults, for both males and females; and the findings of this study apply to children from any family, regardless of the child's initial aggression levels, their intellectual capabilities, their social status as measured by their parents' education or occupation, their parents' aggressiveness, or the mother and father's parenting style.[28] Although much of the research regarding violence in video games mirrors the larger body of work regarding the effects of television violence, there is evidence that the interactive nature of violent video games creates an even greater detrimental effect on the behavior of those who play them than does the passive nature of television or motion pictures.[29] In a joint statement on the impact of video game violence on children, the American Academy of Pediatrics, American Academy of Child and Adolescent Psychiatry, American Psychological Association, American Medical Association, American Academy of Family Physicians, and American Psychiatric Association all declared that the negative effects of interactive entertainment such as video games "may be significantly more severe than that wrought by television, movies, or music."[30] The joint statement also asserts that in some children there is actually a causal connection between video violence and aggressive behavior.[31] Or, as one psychologist put it, "at the most, video games cause children to disregard their natural aversion to killing while at the very least they train children in the art of killing."[32] Others have said that such games "train video game players to shoot and kill in real life."[33]

Besides showing the harmful behavioral effects of violent video games, studies have also demonstrated the ways in which those games are marketed to children. With the average child playing ninety minutes of video games each day,[34] experts estimate that children comprise up to 60 percent of the video game audience.[35] A Federal Trade Commission study released in December of 2001 showed that retailers allowed 78 percent of unaccompanied underage shoppers, including 66 percent of their thirteen-year-old customers, to purchase M-rated games (suitable for persons ages seventeen and older).[36] That same study revealed that 24 percent of children between ages eleven and sixteen included at least one M-rated game when asked to state their three favorite video games.[37] Other studies have found that over 70 percent of M-rated games are marketed to children younger than age seventeen.[38] According to a Federal Trade Commission report, video game manufacturers advertise their most violent games in media most likely to reach young children.[39] The FTC found that the "practice of pervasive and aggressive marketing of violent movies, music and electronic games to children...frustrates parents' attempts to make informed decisions about their children's exposure to violent content."[40]

Undermining the whole point of the ratings system, video game makers "vigorously pursue young, impressionable, alienated" youths as lucrative customers.[41] It markets violent games to young people "especially ill-equipped to deal maturely, responsibly, and safely with the products."[42] As an attempt to further boost its profits, the industry is now striving to "further saturate the preschool market" and to hook girls on violent games.[43]

Not only are the games violent, but their advertisements, apparent to anyone who walks down the video game aisle of a toy store, are filled with violent messages.[44] *Carmageddon* claims it is "as easy as killing babies with axes." *Point Blank* asserts that "it is more fun than shooting your neighbor's cat." And *Die by the Sword* proclaims: "Escape. Dismember. Massacre." Although these are obviously blatant examples, they are indicative of the use of violence to attract buyers. One governmental study found that 89 percent of the M-rated games and 96 percent of the T-rated games had violence-related content descriptors.[45]

Video Game Case Law

In *Interactive Digital*, the Eighth Circuit overruled the lower court's finding that video games were not a protected form of speech.[46] After reviewing four games presented to the court—*Resident Evil*, *Mortal Kombat*, *DOOM*, and *Fear Effect*—U.S. District Judge Stephen Limbaugh concluded that the games convey no "ideas, expression or anything else that could possibly amount to speech."[47] Contrary to the district court's ruling that games needed to "express or inform" before they were entitled to First Amendment protection, the Eighth Circuit held that the First Amendment protects "entertainment, as well as political speech...and that a particularized message is not required for speech to be constitutionally protected."[48] Noting that the First Amendment was versatile enough to protect the paintings of Jackson Pollock and the verse of Lewis Carroll, the court saw no reason why video games should not be entitled to the same protection. It found that the violent video games at issue contained "stories, imagery, [and] age-old themes of literature...just as books and movies do."[49] The court also saw the interactivity of video games as similar to that of literature: "Indeed, literature is most successful when it draws the reader into the story, makes him identify with the characters, invites him to judge them and quarrel with them."[50] Thus, the court concluded, "whether we believe the advent of violent video games adds anything of value to society is irrelevant; guided by the First Amendment, we are obliged to recognize that they are as much entitled to the protection of free speech as the best of literature."[51]

The Eighth Circuit placed great emphasis on its finding that video games possess some kind of storyline, as if this was the vital component of protected speech. In fact, this was really the only element or characteristic of speech mentioned by the court. Though it stated that protected speech was not required to have a particularized message, the court specified no affirmative traits that would have to exist for the First Amendment to apply. It also brushed off any concerns about the violent and sexual images in video games with the comment that "the mere fact that they appear in a novel medium is of no legal consequence."[52] Yet it was almost as if the novelty of the medium served as an automatic qualifier for First Amendment protection, as if the mere newness of video games was enough to warrant full constitutional coverage.

The *Interactive Digital* court relied heavily on a previous Seventh Circuit opinion in *American Amusement Machine Ass'n v. Kendrick* involving a constitutional challenge to an Indianapolis ordinance that sought to limit access of minors to violent video games.[53] In overturning the ordinance and holding that video games qualified for full First Amendment protection, the Seventh Circuit declined to carve out a constitutional exception for violence, such as exists for obscenity.[54] According to the court, obscenity is unprotected not because it affects anyone's conduct (as was alleged in connection with violent video games), but because it violates "community norms regarding the permissible scope of depictions of sexual" activity.[55] Thus, offensiveness, not harmfulness, is why obscenity lacks any constitutional protection. This distinction, the court said, undercut any attempt to carve out a violence exception similar to that of obscenity.[56]

In further support of its opinion, the *Kendrick* court noted that violence is an historic element of cultural expression. "Classic literature and art...are saturated with graphic scenes of violence, whether narrated or pictorial," the court said,[57] likening violent video games to the portrayals of violence in *The Odyssey* (with its graphic descriptions of Odysseus's grinding out the eye of Polyphemus), *The Divine Comedy* (with its graphic descriptions of the tortures of the damned), *War and Peace* (with its graphic descriptions of execution by firing squad), and the stories of Edgar Allen Poe.[58] Violence, according to the court, has always been a central interest of humankind and a recurrent theme of culture; therefore, violent video games are just doing what countless authors have done before. But going even further, the court indicated that such games may be a key component of individual development. According to the court, "people are unlikely to become well-functioning, independent-minded adults and responsible citizens if they are raised in an intellectual bubble."[59] The court asserted that exposure to violent images is something that minors should not be shielded from until they turn eighteen, since it would "not only be quixotic, but deforming" to leave a minor unequipped to cope with the harsh reality of a culture in which violence has become a permanent fixture.[60] Thus, in the court's view, video games are a necessary tool in the nurturing of future citizens and voters, so that young minds "are not a blank when they first exercise the [vote]."[61]

This viewpoint contrasts sharply with that of the D.C. Circuit toward indecent television programming. In upholding FCC rules confining indecent broadcast programming to the hours between 10 p.m. and 6 a.m., the court likewise recognized that a "democratic society rests, for its continuance, upon the healthy, well-rounded growth of young people into full maturity as citizens."[62] But then the court took a completely different approach from that taken in *Kendrick* regarding child development. It upheld legislation shielding children from what was seen to be harmful speech.[63] Furthermore, the court ruled, "a scientific demonstration of psychological harm [is not] required in order to establish the constitutionality of measures protecting minors from exposure to indecent speech."[64] Congress does not need "the testimony of psychiatrists and social scientists in order to take note of the coarsening of impressionable minds that can result from a persistent exposure to sexually explicit material."[65] These same arguments, obviously, could be used in support of regulations limiting minors' access to violent video games.

As with the opinion in *Interactive Digital*, the *Kendrick* decision made numerous presumptions about the speech qualities of video games. In one conclusory paragraph, the court equated video games with the greatest works of literature in human history. It also decided that the interactivity of video games, instead of setting them apart from literature, actually made them more akin to literature. After all, the court noted, it was protests from readers that caused Dickens to revise *Great Expectations* so as to give it a happy ending. As further evidence of the interactivity of literature, the court stated that tourists often visit sites in Dublin where the fictitious events of *Ulysses* are imagined to have occurred.[66] One thing certainly has to be said about the *Kendrick* court: It was definitely getting into the fantasy of fiction when it equated tourists rummaging around neighborhoods in Dublin with young children competing with each other as to how many heads and arms and legs they can blow off with their arsenal of virtual weaponry.

Up until *Kendrick*, no court had explicitly held that video games constituted speech within the meaning of the First Amendment. But subsequently, a number of courts have adopted the *Kendrick* view. In *James v. Meow Media, Inc.*, parents of children killed during a school shooting in Kentucky sued the makers of violent video games that the shooter had frequently played.[67] Following the lead of *Kendrick*, the court ruled that video games were constitutionally protected speech. Just as the *Kendrick* court had done, the *James* court refused to extend the obscenity exception beyond material of a sexual nature.[68] It did not even consider carving out a new violence exception to protected speech. Even though video games are a relatively new medium, and even though they contain violence of a uniquely graphic nature, the court declined to examine whether such violence should be treated as obscenity—that is, as speech outside the scope of the First Amendment. In the current media environment, however, with the explosion of graphics imagery and simulated reality, it makes sense to take a fresh look at what kinds of "entertainment" should receive constitutional protection and what should be given a lesser degree of constitutional status.

The Shift in Judicial Treatment

The first video game cases were fairly uniform in their denial of First Amendment protections. In *America's Best Family Showplace v. City of New York,* the court likened video games to mechanical entertainment devices, such as pinball machines, and recreational pastimes, such as chess and baseball, consisting of rules and implements:

> In no sense can it be said that video games are meant to inform.... That some of these games talk to the participant, play music, or have written instructions does not provide the missing element of information.... [T]hey contain so little in the way of particularized form of expression that video games cannot be fairly characterized as a form of speech protected by the First Amendment.[69]

The court required that for entertainment speech to be constitutionally protected it had to contain a communicative or informative element.[70]

Subsequent to the *America's Best* decision, other courts followed suit and held that since video games were not designed to communicate or express information, they could not receive constitutional protection.[71] In *Carswell*, for instance, the Massachusetts Supreme Court held that any communication of information disseminated while playing a video game is inconsequential.[72] But this approach to video games all changed with the *Kendrick* decision.

Although the Seventh Circuit held that violence did not fit into the unique niche occupied by obscenity within First Amendment jurisprudence,[73] it refused to consider whether a particular form of violence (video game violence) should be given its own category of First Amendment exclusion. Nor did the court consider whether obscenity should be given a more expansive reading beyond mere offensiveness. But contrary to the court's reasoning, the rationale for obscenity laws goes beyond simply the offensive nature of the material. In *Paris Adult Theatre v. Slaton*, for instance, the Supreme Court suggested that a connection between antisocial behavior and obscene material could also justify legislative regulation of obscenity.[74]

The *Kendrick* approach also erodes the integrity of the constitutional model governing the broadcast medium. If broadcast content can be regulated based on the fact that the broadcast medium has the capacity to be intrusive and harmful to children in ways that the print media is not, then other new media should be similarly treated if found to have that harmful or manipulative characteristic. But when the courts automatically elevate violent video games, in a First Amendment sense, above that of the broadcast medium, the entire rationale underlying broadcast regulation is cast into doubt.

Another criticism of the *Kendrick* opinion involves its view of video games as a type of speech vital to human development. The Seventh Circuit, in comparing the restrictions on video games with Nazi Germany's denial of free speech to children, states that violence has always been a part of society and that children should not be shielded from it, lest they be left "unequipped to cope with the world as we know it."[75] The court also compared the violence in video games with that portrayed in some of the great works of literature. But to say that the descriptions of violence in *The Odyssey*, *The Divine Comedy*, and *War and Peace* are similar to the violent imagery in video games is to stretch reality to the breaking point. Despite the court's characterization of literature as an interactive medium, a book is nowhere near as interactive as a video game. And certainly no book seeks to make the violence as addicting and all-consuming as do video games. Because of technological developments, modern video games are capable of portraying violence in a graphic, thrilling, and even appealing way that books cannot come close to replicating.[76]

If the *Kendrick* court is correct in its view that children, so as to develop into healthy, mature adults, need to be exposed to violence through some media form, then wouldn't it be wiser to steer this exposure toward the medium of books and newspapers? Is not the print medium a place where individuals get a more informed, broad-based, and less sensationalized education on a subject such as social violence? Isn't the print medium a preferred medium for that kind of educational and developmental purpose? Shouldn't courts, in a media society such as America has become, look to the totality of the speech available to the public? Since violence is so pervasively expressed through every medium in society, is it really a constitutional violation to limit its expression or conveyance in just one of the media outlets operating in a media-abundant society?

The Judicial Duty to Define Protected Speech

As America, the world leader in entertainment media, increasingly specializes its economy toward its strengths, more and more different kinds of technological imagery and graphics and entertainment will be developed, and each of these will inevitably seek constitutional protection. As courts have asserted, "there is no precise test for determining how the First Amendment protects a given form of expression."[77] Each medium "must be assessed for First Amendment purposes by standards suited to it, for each may present its own problems."[78] These statements seem to reflect precisely what the First Amendment requires: for judges to closely scrutinize the communicative aspects of new media before granting constitutional protection. But instead, in the case of video games, the courts have all followed the *Kendrick* lead and held that any medium that simply "evokes emotions by imagery" falls under the First Amendment.[79] Under this approach, there is nothing to stop amusement park thrill-houses to receive constitutional protection, since they too "evoke emotions by imagery." Furthermore, despite the assertion that any medium that evokes emotions by imagery qualifies for full First Amendment protections, not all forms of media do receive such protections. The broadcast media, for instance, occupies a lower constitutional status than does the print medium; and the content of broadcast speech can be more easily regulated than can the content of newspapers.[80]

The line of recent video game cases seems to rest constitutional protection on the artistic creativity embodied in the software, rather than upon any communication of ideas. But if artistic creativity is the essential component of protected speech, then shouldn't the color schemes and furniture arrangements of interior designers qualify for First Amendment protections? The cases also seem to rely on the realism that the games are able to convey. Sophisticated games today use full-motion video, detailed animation, and stereo surround sound to bring their action to life. But if simulating reality is a component of First Amendment coverage, then shouldn't the sets and targets in a realistic shooting range qualify for constitutional protection?

The video game industry is a behemoth. Sales of video game software in the United States alone amounted to almost $7 billion in 2005.[81] Contrary to the realities existing when Justice Holmes first articulated his marketplace metaphor, the video game industry is not a speaker facing insurmountable odds in putting its political speech into the public domain. It is not a speaker in desperate need of constitutional protection, lest its "messages" be erased by an intolerant society. Even if violent video games were regulated, the industry would continue to thrive. The pornography industry provides an instructive analogy on this point: Despite decades of zoning restrictions and the threat of obscenity prosecutions, pornography remains highly profitable and pervasive. The only real hope is that the most dangerous and destructive products of the video game industry can be channeled so as to diminish the extent of the destructiveness. As Professor Kunich observes about the industry:

> Rather than marginalized, unpopular political speech aimed at changing significant portions of American government or society, [video games are] nonpolitical, commercially sold entertainment that is aggressively marketed for appeal to a mass audience, usually comprised of minors, to sell as many copies as possible of the work in question. In sharp contrast to the aim of shaping the political direction of the nation, [video games] are at least primarily, if not exclusively, designed to appeal to the tastes of a particular segment of consumers, so as to earn as much revenue as possible for the creators, producers, and distributors of that type of entertainment.... In sharp contrast to

the archetype of anathematized political activists struggling to convey their message to even a few receptive listeners, [video game makers] are typically prosperous objects of adulation in their chosen market niche and often reach hundreds of thousands, and even millions, of paying consumers with each new product, [which uses] outrageous violence and strongly antisocial themes [as] powerful selling points.... Generally, less mature adolescent or near-adolescent males comprise the market segment that favors the most rebellious shocking forms of entertainment.... Rational business judgment moves some entertainers and their marketing support structure to attempt to cater to this lucrative consumer base with material that shocks authority figures and reinforces the customers' defiant self-image.... [But] the definition of "shocking" is a moving target. Material that is on the fringe at one point in time quickly becomes assimilated into the boring mainstream in the opinion of the youthful consumers, and so the purveyors of shocking entertainment must continually exert themselves to stretch the boundaries of acceptability further.... Thus, over time, the trend inexorably leads towards increasingly graphic, sociopathic blood sports.[82]

Applying the marketplace model to video games is inherently contradictory, because the makers of video games are nothing like the "street corner speakers" initially envisioned by Justice Holmes. Moreover, the "speech" of video games is nothing like the kind of speech meant to be protected by the Framers. Video games do not come close to meeting the definition of political speech offered in the preceding chapter. Despite all this, however, the courts have unthinkingly extended First Amendment protection to the most violent of imagery contained in those games. They have not even considered whether to characterize video game content as a kind of lower-value speech, entitled merely to some degree of constitutional coverage. In *Watters v. TSR, Inc.*, the court held that regardless of whether a certain video game was characterized as literature or merely a game, it nonetheless fell within the category of protected speech.[83] However, no analysis was provided as to why the game constituted protected speech. This stance was similar to the one later taken in the *Kendrick* and *James* cases, where the courts adopted an absolutist position that all video games, even if designed solely to entertain, are not only a protected form of expression but are entitled to the same level of protection as political speech.[84]

Under the First Amendment, there is no deference or benefit of the doubt given to the initial decision—that of whether something qualifies as protected speech—as there is to the second decision—whether particular restrictions on protected speech are allowed to stand. Consequently, judges should take a more critical stance toward examining the constitutional worthiness of new forms of media. They should adopt a "defining in" approach, which "would identify a category of covered speech based upon the underlying theory of the First Amendment and would exclude everything else."[85] But as one commentator has put it, modern First Amendment doctrine has followed a "defining out" approach, whereby speech is presumptively within the realm of the First Amendment unless it is shown to be excluded."[86] The video game cases reflect this trend of adopting a presumption of constitutional protection to new forms of media content, even though there is nothing in First Amendment jurisprudence that commands the judiciary to make this presumption. To the contrary, when new kinds of speech or media are in issue, it should be the burden of the speaker to show that such speech qualifies for First Amendment protections.

It has been thirty years since the Court last created an exception to protected speech under the First Amendment.[87] Perhaps the media and technological developments of the past three decades should now warrant either a violence exception or a completely new approach to determining what kind of speech is protected by the First Amendment.

With respect to determining what speech is to be protected under the First Amendment, courts have found an "elusive line between entertaining and informing."[88] But instead of trying to address or determine this elusive line, they have simply fallen back upon a presumption of protected speech. They have not articulated a coherent theory or any set of factors that might ever justify not extending constitutional protection.[89] Consequently, we have been left with the rule that practically any form of entertainment will be viewed as protected speech.

This approach, however, poses problems when viewed within the larger context of the media society that America has become. Contrary to the situation of even twenty or thirty years ago, the advance of communications technologies has brought on an explosion of different kinds and forms of entertainment. If the courts cannot somehow carve out of this dense forest of entertainment a clearing of First Amendment speech, then the First Amendment itself will increasingly lose meaning, not amidst censorship, but amidst a suffocating blanket of media chatter. Because as the twenty-first century gets underway, the real censorship danger to political speech is an indirect censorship—a censorship caused by the flood of entertainment that threatens to choke out political speech. And the courts contribute to this indirect censorship if they fail to closely scrutinize any new forms of media content that make a claim for speech protection under the First Amendment.

Notes

1. *Interactive Digital Software Ass'n v. St. Louis County, Missouri*, 329 F.3d 954 (8th Cir. 2003).
2. Ibid., 958.
3. John H. Garvey and Frederick Schauer, eds., *The First Amendment: A Reader* (Eagan, MN: West Publishing, 1996), 100 (stating that "if we define [free speech] too broadly we will weaken the First Amendment protection by spreading it too thin").
4. "Illinois Governor Wants Video-Game Ban," *Fox News*, December 16, 2004, at www.foxnews.com/printer_friendly_story/0,3566,141705,00.html.
5. *James v. Meow Media, Inc.*, 90 F. Supp.2d 798 (W.D. Ky. 2000).
6. *Golden v. State*, 21 S.W.3d 801 (Ark. 2000).
7. *State v. Kinkel*, 56 P.3d 463 (Or. Ct. App. 2002).
8. Bill Dedman, "Bullying, Tormenting Often Led to Revenge in Cases Studied," *Chicago Sun-Times*, Oct. 15, 2000, 14.
9. *Sanders v. Acclaim Entm't, Inc.*, 188 F. Supp.2d 1264, 1268 (D. Colo. 2002).
10. *Sanders*, 188 F. Supp.2d 1264, 1269.
11. Dave Grossman and Gloria Degaetano, *Stop Teaching Our Kids to Kill: A Call to Action Against TV, Movie and Video Game Violence* (New York: Crown, 1999), 111.
12. Scott Whittier, "School Shootings: Are Video Game Manufacturers Doomed to Tort Liability?" 17 *Whittier Entertainment & Sports Law* 11, 14-15 (2000); Richard C. Ausness, "The Application of Product Liability Principles to Publishers of Violent or Sexually Explicit Material," 52 *Florida Law Review* 603, 604-07 (2000).
13. Whittier, "School Shootings," 13-14.
14. Federal Trade Commission, *Marketing Violent Entertainment to Children: A Review of Self-Regulation and Industry Practices in the Motion Picture, Music Recording & Electronic Game Industries.* Appendix A: "A Review of Research on the Impact of Violence in Entertainment Media" (September, 2000), 12 [hereinafter *FTC Violence Rpt.*].
15. Anita Hamilton, "Video Vigilantes," *TIME*, January 10, 2005, 60.
16. *Marketing Violence to Children: Hearing Before the Senate Comm. On Commerce, Science, and Transp.*, App. A, 4-5,12, 106th Cong. (2000) [hereinafter *Marketing Violence*]; see also Scott A. Pyle, "Is Violence Really Just Fun and Games? A Proposal for a Violent Video Game Ordinance that Passes Constitutional Muster," 37 *Valparaiso University Law Review* 429, 430 (2002).
17. *Marketing Violence*, 12.
18. Ibid., 2.
19. John Charles Kunich, "Natural Born Copycat Killers and the Law of Shock Torts," 78 *Washington University Law Quarterly* 1157, 1159 (2000).
20. Susan Vaughan, "What Makes Children Kill?" *Harper's Bazaar,* September 1998, 546.
21. Peter Schweizer, "Bad Imitation," *National Review*, December 1998, 23.
22. Ibid.
23. Ibid.
24. Kunich, "Natural Born Copycat Killers and the Law of Shock Torts," 1162.
25. Chuck Philips, "Gangsta Rap: Did Lyrics Inspire Killing of Police?" *Los Angeles Times,* October 17, 1994, F2.
26. Joel Timmer, "When a Commercial is not a Commercial: Advertising of Violent Entertainment and the First Amendment," 7 *Communications Law and Policy* 157, 167 (2002).

27. Ibid.
28. L. R. Huesmann et al., "Longitudinal Relations Between Children's Exposure to TV Violence and their Aggressive and Violent Behavior in Young Adulthood," 39 *Developmental Psychology* 201 (2003).
29. Craig A. Anderson, *The Impact of Interactive Violence on Children*, Congressional Testimony, March 21, 2000, 2000 WL 11070122, 3-5.
30. American Academy Of Pediatrics, *Joint Statement on the Impact of Entertainment Violence on Children, Congressional Public Health Summit* 2 (July 26, 2000).
31. Ibid.
32. Kevin E. Barton, "Game Over! Legal Response to Video Game Violence," 16 *Notre Dame Journal of Law, Ethics & Pubic Policy* 133, 143 (2002).
33. Tara Campbell, "Did Video Games Train the School Shooters to Kill?" 84 *Marquette Law Review* 811, 814 (2001).
34. *Marketing Violence*, 1 (testimony of Donald E. Cook). A survey by Michigan State University found that eighth-grade boys play video games on average twenty-three hours a week. Hamilton, "Video Vigilantes," 63.
35. *FTC Violence Rpt.*, App. D, 5.
36. Federal Trade Commission, *Marketing Violent Entertainment to Children*, 33 (December 2001).
37. Ibid,, 47.
38. Campbell, "Did Video Games Train the School Shooters to Kill?" 818.
39. Timmer, "When a Commercial is not a Commercial," 158.
40. Ibid., 158-59.
41. Kunich, "Natural Born Copycat Killers and the Law of Shock Torts," 1254, 1244.
42. Ibid., 1249.
43. Jonathan Dee, "Playing Mogul," *New York Times Magazine*, December 21, 2003, 40.
44. *Marketing Violence to Children: Hearing Before the Senate Comm. On Commerce, Science, and Transp.*, 106th Cong. (1999) (testimony of Sen. Joe Lieberman).
45. *FTC Violence Rpt.*, App. D, 5. Games rated "Teen (T)" have content suitable for persons ages thirteen and older.
46. *Interactive Digital Software Ass'n v. St. Louis County*, 200 F. Supp.2d 1126, 1135 (E.D. Mo. 2002).
47. Ibid., 1132.
48. *Interactive*, 329 F.3d 957.
49. Ibid.
50. Ibid.
51. Ibid., 958.
52. Ibid., 957.
53. *American Amusement Machine Ass'n. v. Kendrick*, 244 F.3d 572 (7th Cir. 2001).
54. Ibid., 574 (citing *R.A.V. v. City of St. Paul*, 505 U.S. 377, 382 (1992)).
55. Ibid.
56. Ibid.
57. Ibid.
58. Ibid., 577.
59. Ibid; see also David C. Kiernan, "Shall the Sins of the Son Be Visited Upon the Father? Video Game Manufacturer Liability for Violent Video Games," 52 *Hastings Law Journal* 207, 219 (2000) (arguing that "not recognizing video games as a form of protected entertainment deprives citizens access to aesthetic, political, social, moral, and other ideas and experiences that are or may be intertwined with the video game").

60. *American Amusement Machine Ass'n*, 244 F.3d 577-8.
61. Ibid., 577.
62. *Action for Children's Television v. FCC*, 58 F.3d 654, 661 (D.C. Cir. 1995).
63. Ibid.
64. Ibid., 662.
65. Ibid., 662-3 (adding that the "Supreme Court has reminded us that society has an interest not only in the health of its youth, but also in its quality").
66. *American Amusement Machine Ass'n*, 244 F.3d 577.
67. *James v. Meow Media, Inc.*, 300 F.3d 683 (6th Cir. 2002).
68. Ibid., 697.
69. *America's Best Family Showplace Corp. v. City of New York*, 536 F.Supp. 170, 174 (E.D.N.Y. 1982).
70. Ibid., 173.
71. *Malden Amusement Co., Inc. v. City of Malden*, 582 F. Supp. 297, 299 (D.C. Mass. 1983); *Kaye v. Planning & Zoning Comm'n*, 472 A.2d 809, 810 (Conn. Super. Ct. 1983); *Caswell v. Licensing Comm'n for Brockton*, 444 N.E.2d 922, 925 (Mass. 1983); *Marshfield Family Skateland, Inc. v. Town of Marshfield*, 450 N.E.2d 605, 609 (Mass. 1983); *People v. Walker*, 354 N.W.2d 312, 316 (Mich. Ct. App. 1984); *City of St. Louis v. Kiely*, 652 S.W.2d 694, 696 (Mo. Ct. App. 1983); *Tommy & Tina, Inc. v. Dep't of Consumer Affairs*, 459 N.Y.S.2d 220, 226 (N.Y. Sup. Ct. 1983).
72. *Carswell*, 444 N.E.2d 922, 927 (1983).
73. *American Amusement Machine Ass'n*, 244 F.3d 574-5.
74. *Paris Adult Theatre I v. Slaton*, 413 U.S. 49, 60 (1973).
75. *American Amusement Machine Ass'n*, 244 F.3d 577.
76. William Li, "Unbaking the Adolescent Cake: The Constitutional Implications of Imposing Tort Liability on Publishers of Violent Video Games," 45 *Arizona Law Review* 467, 476 (2003).
77. *Wilson v. Midway Games, Inc.*, 198 F. Supp. 2d 167, 179 (D. Conn. 2002) (involving a personal injury claim against the video game industry).
78. Ibid.; *Southeastern Productions, Inc. v. Conrad*, 420 U.S. 546, 557 (1975).
79. *Wilson*, 198 F. Supp.2d at 181.
80. *FCC v. Pacifica Foundation*, 438 U.S. 726, 748-51 (1978); *Red Lion Broadcasting Co. v. FCC*, 395 U.S. 367 (1969).
81. Hamilton, "Video Vigilantes," 60.
82. Kunich, "Natural Born Copycat Killers and the Law of Shock Torts," 1225-27.
83. 715 F. Supp. 819, 820 (W.D. Ky. 1989), *aff'd on other grounds*, *Watters v. TSR*, 904 F. 2d 378 (6th Cir. 1990).
84. Kiernan, "Shall the Sins of the Son be Visited Upon the Father?" 215.
85. Cynthia L. Estland, "Speech on Matters of Public Concern: The Perils of an Emerging First Amendment Category," 59 *George Washington Law Review* 1, 41 (1990).
86. Ibid.
87. *Miller v. California*, 413 U.S. 15, 24 (1973).
88. Kiernan, "Shall the Sins of the Son Be Visited Upon the Father?" 217.
89. Ibid.

Conclusion: The First Amendment in a Media-Saturated Society

A Constitutional Shield for America's Mega-Industry

Under the marketplace model, the First Amendment free speech guaranty has become a shield for the often libertine behavior of the modern media. Any government inquiry or any public outrage is answered with a self-righteous recitation of America's most famous constitutional provision. To listen to media spokespersons defend decadent entertainment is to hear lofty pronouncements of individual freedom, constitutional heritage, and the evils of government tyranny. To listen to the media defend how it earns its living is to hear the same words used by Chinese dissidents who sacrifice their lives for the cause of freedom and democracy.

The media claims to be the defender of the First Amendment, but it has long since lost touch with any First Amendment reality. In its world of paranoia-laced fantasy, it sees any social attempt to impose accountability on it as a dark plot to subvert the Constitution. It sees any public reaction against its most offensive output as the beachhead landing of an unenlightened enemy bent on forcing America into a cultural stone age. After the FCC cracked down on broadcast indecency following Janet Jackson's breast-baring incident during the 2004 Super Bowl halftime show, the media cried that it was being targeted by the forces of intolerant "prudishness."[1] How laughable, to think that any reasonable observer could believe that the American media was being subverted by "prudishness." And obviously, Hollywood celebrities did not feel too besieged, since in 2004 at a political fundraiser a number of them belittled President Bush with crude and vulgar jokes.

When a radio network dropped the Howard Stern show after being hit with a hefty fine for Stern's indecent language, Hollywood complained that the FCC's actions were sending "shock-waves through the industry."[2] Because they might not be entirely free to

147

produce the kind of disgusting dialogue that Howard Stern spews out, "talented writers, producers and actors [would] flee broadcast television," it was predicted.[3] But then, how talented could they be if they could not rise above the level of Howard Stern?

All the usual media defenses have become so familiar that they seem to permanently echo within society. Offensive lyrics, claims a chairman of Time Warner Music Group, are "the price you pay for freedom of expression."[4] No, offensive lyrics are the price that is paid for a music industry profiteering off impressionable and rebellious youths. For more than two hundred years, freedom has existed in America without anything even remotely close to the kind of offensive speech existing today. "We're just satisfying the consumer demand," media officials say, justifying the violence and sexual exploitation. But so is the cocaine dealer, and the illegal arms supplier—they too are just supplying a demand. History proves that there is always a desire for destructive and decadent products, yet the whole purpose of several thousand years of civilization has been to control that demand.

"Television programming simply reflects reality," network executives argue. But according to studies, two percent of all the characters appearing on television each night are murdered.[5] If this rate occurred in reality, however, the entire U.S. population would be killed off in fifty days. Another study found that the more people from other countries watched American television programs, the more negative their perceptions were of Americans.[6]

"If it is so offensive, then you don't need to see it or listen to it," media executives pronounce, in reply to protests over their offensive products. But in a media-drenched society, this reply is a little like telling people protesting river pollution that they don't need to drink the water. Even if a person never buys a video game or music recording, they will still be living in a society whose moral and aesthetic environment has been degraded and brutalized. Most arguments opposing offensive speech focus on its effects on children, but the degradation and obscenity produced by the media taints people of all ages; it taints an entire culture.

"It's not our job to supervise children; it's the parents' job," proclaim television executives, in answer to complaints about programming that is clearly inappropriate for children. But the problem is, many parents are unable to adequately supervise, and the television industry knows it. Besides, if this defense is acceptable, then why is there such a demand for safety-locks on guns that parents have in the house. Why have a safety-lock? Shouldn't it just be up to the parents to supervise their children?

"Live and uncensored programming is the hallmark of a free society," television producers claim.[7] So, a society in which reading and civilized political debate are becoming extinct and in which violence is a constant danger is a free society just because of "The Bachelor," "Fear Factor," and "Survivor." Perhaps that was what should have been done in Iraq. Forget the schools and the polling places and the security police: The way to freedom was through live and uncensored television.

Whenever the media comes under public criticism, it invokes the protecting hand of the First Amendment. But despite all the shallow and trite defenses asserted by the media, the First Amendment was not intended as a legal shield to one industry, protecting it from the kinds of liability that makers of tennis shoes and soft drinks must incur. The First Amendment was not adopted so that media corporations could reap huge profits while passing off disgusting entertainment to a public long manipulated into accepting it.

When the city of Cincinnati initiated an obscenity prosecution against the museum that displayed Robert Mapplethorpe's photographs, including one of a crucifix standing in a jar of urine and titled "Piss of Christ," it was ridiculed in the media for being backward and repressive. One cartoonist depicted a sleazy figure huddled in a Cincinnati alley trying to sell "feelthy pictures" to passing pedestrians.[8] The picture was a reproduction of a Michelangelo. And that is the arrogance of the media: to liken Mapplethorpe to Michelangelo.

The media argues that any attempt by the public to control the amount of vulgarity and violence in popular entertainment will suffocate all creativity and originality. But history contradicts this claim. The 1930s and 1940s, when the Hays Office acted as a nongovernmental censor on Hollywood, is known as the golden age of movies. And the supposedly conservative 1950s, when Rod Serling and Reginald Rose wrote edgy, compelling adult drama without the aid of graphic violence and sexual exploitation, is often called the golden age of television. What these historical examples illustrate is that good art is not suppressed by notions of public decency, but by the debauched sensibilities of a culture that has been barraged by so much repulsive speech that it no longer can appreciate nuance, subtlety, or beauty.

What the media never admits is that it uses toilet humor and bloody violence and loads of sex because it's easier that way; it's easier than creating captivating, touching stories. As comedian and TV veteran Carol Burnett observes, the "loosening of network strictures about language and sex has not necessarily stirred the creativity of television and comedy writers"; instead, it may have made them lazier.[9] "I'm not a prude at all, but I get a little tired when you watch sitcoms and you know there's going to be another sex joke," she says.[10] "How many do you have to hear before you say, 'Please, can you change the subject?'"

The First Amendment is not being subverted by those who are trying to slow the media's freefall into filth and decadence: It is being subverted by a media hiding its culture-corrupting content behind simplistic and irrelevant free speech defenses. And because of this diversionary ruse, because of the continued use of an outmoded marketplace model, the courts are ignoring the real crisis that has arisen with the First Amendment.

A Crisis of Culture and Community

In a court decision granting free speech protections to a rap artist whose lyrics were both violent and pornographic, the judge nonetheless condemned the lyrics as "both disgusting and offensive" and stated that the artist's popularity was "an indication of society's aesthetic and moral decay."[11] But the fact that a judge feels helpless to do anything but automatically apply the First Amendment to almost any speech at issue is itself a sign that the free speech clause has drifted into some unknown and unnavigable universe.

Elsewhere in the law, community interests are thriving. The communal interest in diversity and racial harmony has allowed the courts to override the Equal Protection clause with regard to affirmative action programs, and the communal interest in social order and law enforcement has prompted courts to declare that religious exercise rights cannot trump neutral laws that are generally applicable to everyone. However, when it comes to speech and the media, the community has virtually no power.

Rudyard Kipling believed that civilization was something laboriously achieved yet only precariously defended. Though, if nothing defines a civilization better than the state of its public discourse, then America is not even precariously defending its own civilization. According to Professor Heyman, "the community should have the power to uphold standards of civility within the public sphere."[12] But whenever they are confronted with this notion of civility and communal standards, media executives paint a lurid picture of being stalked by the "decency police"; they conjure up images of the Inquisition or a Salem witch-hunt. Perhaps there is reason for Hollywood to fear decency; but what reason does the rest of society have for trembling at the word? Besides, all the exaggerated and paranoid claims about "decency police" are just plain ridiculous. Decency in the public media died long ago, and people are trying not so much to re-impose it as they are trying to contain the *in*decency within whatever limits they can achieve.

Decency is often depicted by free-speech advocates as something dark and threatening—as the unmistakable trait of an intolerant past. But there is no historical evidence of a free society ever collapsing, or even being weakened, by any public code of decency. Indeed, just the opposite is true. Tyranny and chaos ensue whenever societies abandon any adherence to decency standards. Moreover, a society that thinks the freedom of an entire nation may be threatened by the imposition of certain social constraints on the distribution of popular entertainment products—like a music video in which an angry young male simulates sex with his mother[13]—is a society that has taken individual narcissism and nihilism to a fanatical end.

Free-speech absolutists dwell on only one side of the censorship issue: the power of the community to coerce individual (or more accurately, corporate media) speech. They ignore the flipside of the issue: the power of unconstrained entertainment speech to corrode a civilized culture. But how can a society be free if it lacks the ability to reject what it deems harmful and despicable? How can it be free if it is not free from the decadence and bad taste of a few? How can it be free if it is powerless to stop the coarsening of its culture by a profit-gorging entertainment industry? Indeed, some critics claim that the most harmful effect of media violence is not the occurrence of violent behavior but a coarsened culture of disrespect, which in turn leads to a moral indifference.

During the 1990s, the advocates of "political correctness" sought to reform cultural vocabulary in an effort to reform cultural attitudes. To combat sexism, "spokesman" was changed to "spokesperson." To combat belittling stereotypes, "mentally retarded" was changed to "mentally challenged"; "cripple" was replaced by "physically handicapped." These changes recognize the fact that language has power, that language can affect attitudes, and that attitudes can affect action. When hate-speech codes were implemented at universities, the sponsors implicitly admitted that if bounds were not placed on a culture's speech, then speech could not be used to place bounds on a culture's actions. Free speech can hardly build civic virtue and racial justice if so much of that speech is vile.

Every civilized culture must be governed by some standard of civic prudence, some ability to constrain its latent vices and keep its indulgences and weaknesses in check. It is this act of restraint that produces true freedom—a freedom to reach beyond self-gratification, a freedom that separates child from adult, animal from human. How historically ignorant it is to bombard young people, who have difficulty enough controlling their own hormones, with rampant sexual entertainment, and yet at the same time expect them to avoid pregnancy and sexually-transmitted diseases and emotional breakdown, all the while maturing into socially-concerned, public-interested, well-educated citizens.

Alexander Bickel wrote that speech was only free in a democracy if it was conducted within certain bounds of civility.[14] This decorum argument was undoubtedly a foregone conclusion with the framers: that all public speech, even if free from government restraint, would be expressed within the parameters of respect, civility, and decorum; and that the First Amendment was in no way aimed at erasing these customs. He believed that a democratic community could enact certain speech-constraining laws if necessary to sustain "the style and quality of life minimally congenial to them."[15] According to Bickel, these laws might also be necessitated by the breakdown of many social customs that formerly served as a kind of unofficial cultural censor, imposing a framework of civility on public speech. It is for just this reason, to counteract the media's drift away from these customs of decorum, that the public needs some tool to help it revive a sense of social civility—something akin to a private right to censor, belonging to every member of society.

The media's contorted use of the marketplace model has enabled a libertine, irresponsible individualism to trump a culture's sense of decency. This poses a grave risk to freedom, argues Professor Stanley Brubaker, because it is the character of citizens that ultimately influences the course of a democratic society.[16] Yet the constant media bombardment of indecency is steadily grinding down the sensitivities of society. More than a decade ago, public protests forced the designer Calvin Klein to cancel an ad campaign depicting teenagers in sexually provocative poses: In one, an adolescent girl was pictured lying down, lifting her skirt. Tipper Gore, before her husband needed campaign funds from Hollywood, led a crusade to clean up music lyrics. In the 1960s, Newton Minow likened television to a wasteland, and, in 1973, one media observer wrote that "one of these days people are going to turn against television instead of turning it on."[17] But over the years, this social opposition to television has been gradually worn down. Now, the public seems to have given up, to have acquiesced to most of the corrosive media influences; now, the public only wants to try to "manage" the degree to which these influences invade their family's life. But the marketplace model will not even allow that concession to the besieged.

In 1942, the Supreme Court unanimously held that certain speech should not be constitutionally protected because of its destructive effect on social "morality."[18] Today, however, courts would have a very difficult time in holding up public morality as a counterweight to even the most repulsive of music lyrics or video graphics. In *Paris Adult Theater I v. Slaton*, the Court acknowledged that states can regulate not only health and safety but also "the morality of the community." Yet, over the years, this interest in public morality has been totally submerged by a First Amendment doctrine that elevates the most disgusting and offensive entertainment messages over any concern for society's moral health. The marketplace model has become a tool in the cause of moral relativism and cultural nihilism.

The freedom and ability to censor can be a powerful means in advancing the reach of civilization. It can also help the individual reach the highest levels of self-fulfillment and personal autonomy. Contrary to the current messages of the mass media, individual fulfillment has not been historically measured by the indulgence of those temptations. Instead, human achievement has been cast in terms of rising above temptations, undisciplined desires, and self-indulgences. To a person trying to lose weight, the constant presence of candy bars and potato chips is not a helpful thing. To that person, those appetite temptations represent not a freedom but a constant threat of enslavement to one's weaknesses. So too is it with much of the media entertainment today: It is not an invitation to personal growth, but a temptation to indulge one's baser instincts. According to some observers, the media-driven patterns of self-indulgence and

self-involvement "are steadily breaking down the habits of restraint
and responsibility" on which democracy depends.[19]

As Roger Shattuck has written, "all of us can feel and have felt
this tug toward what is vile, and have yielded to it in varying degrees, [but] the fragile compact we live by declares that we should
not follow these impulses too often or too far."[20] And as Stephen
Carter observes:

> All of us have a baser side to our natures, and the appeal to what is worst in us is the
> source of the pornographer's profits. Sometimes television programming, too, appeals
> to the bad part of our nature, which is not what civility demands. To advertise hard to
> stimulate demand is, in this context, like offering a bribe. The fact that a person might
> take the bribe is no evidence that the bribe itself is a good thing.[21]

Because so much of contemporary media entertainment appeals to
the baser side of human nature, the freedom of individuals to censor
or remove this temptation is a freedom consistent with the highest
ideals of humanity. Seen in this light, the entertainment products of
the media industry do not reflect free speech as much as they do a
disrespect for the nobility of the human spirit. They reflect not the
opinions of "street corner speakers," but a manipulative enticement
for people to cast off the historic norms of civilized society. Consequently, private censorship can represent an attempt to practice the
age-old virtue of self-restraint—a virtue ignored if not belittled in
today's media culture. It can represent a way of screening out the
temptations that so often divert the quest to become virtuous. To the
constitutional framers, one of the roles of government was to cultivate a sense of civic virtue by helping individuals avoid the indulgence of private passions.[22] The facilitation of a private right to censor would probably qualify as such a role.

The entertainment media plays to the undeliberative impulses of
people's vulnerabilities to distraction. Sitting down in a rocking chair
at the end of a long day, one's mind is all too easily consumed with
the unthinking, hypnotic images on the television screen. But just
because one watches those images at that particular moment does
not mean that such a decision is the product of either a rational choice
or one's best intentions. The real issue is: What would that same
person choose in a moment of untempted rationality? Every parent
in the world knows that a bowl full of candy sitting out on the kitchen
counter prior to dinner will prompt certain actions, but every parent
also knows that such actions are not the wisest or most productive
decisions that could be made in the absence of that candy.

The ability of the media to addict and manipulate is reflected by the power of mass media advertising. It "waters down values, wears them out by slow attrition, makes them banal and, in the long run, helps Americans become indifferent to them and even cynical."[23] Advertising, as does all of the electronic mass media, fosters a "live-for-the-moment" mindset.[24] It is a mindset devoid of logic or rationality.[25] Moreover, it is advertisers who are regarded as the principal customers of the mass media, which in turn sees the public as simply a manipulable audience to be delivered up to advertisers.[26]

A censorship of temptations represents the freedom to make choices in a rational moment and consistent with one's highest goals, rather than succumbing to emotional reactions that are often the result of manipulative and addictive media influences. It represents the freedom to avoid being trapped in a media tidal wave that can otherwise flood one's world and overpower one's ability to swim to shore.

If the function of politics in a civic republican system is "to provide opportunities for preference formation rather than simply to implement existing desires," then the freedom to exercise disciplined and well-intentioned choices provided by a private right to censor fulfills the most basic function of democratic society.[27] But if, on the other hand, individuals become so tainted by the manipulative messages of the mass media that they can no longer freely choose their speech intake, then they have become not only less autonomous as individuals but less trustworthy as democratic citizens and voters.[28]

A More Realistic View of Individual Freedom

The courts have allowed government to regulate a host of constitutional rights. Campaign speech can be regulated, as can firearm ownership. When laws infringe on religious exercise, the courts in most instances do not even strictly scrutinize those laws. And of course, property rights have long been regulated.

During the eighteenth and nineteenth centuries, perhaps the most cherished of constitutional rights were property and economic rights. As countless historians have theorized, the underlying purpose of both the Revolutionary War and the drafting of the U.S. Constitution was the preservation of property rights. Indeed, in an age when people's livelihoods derived from the land or artisan businesses they operated, the protection of property rights was akin to the preservation of life and family.

Property rights reigned supreme with the judiciary throughout the nineteenth century and into the twentieth. But then the courts shifted direction. In the New Deal-era decisions that overruled *Lochner v. New York*,[29] the Supreme Court struck down the supremacy of property rights and upheld the state's freedom to regulate those rights.[30] Since 1937, the Court has abandoned almost all constitutional limits on government regulation of economic affairs, even though property rights were once seen to be more fundamental than First Amendment freedoms.[31] This relaxed judicial stance toward economic liberty reflects the belief that unregulated economic activity can infringe on the freedom of many people in the economic marketplace.[32] A similar stance, according to some scholars, should be taken toward speech. Professor Sunstein, for instance, argues that government should be as free to decide when certain media conditions or speech behavior threaten "harmful consequences for free expression" as it is to determine when particular activities in the oil industry threaten harmful consequences for other industries or consumers.[33]

The private-right-to-censor theory in a way follows the pattern of property rights. There are some rights that are so vital to a free society that they cannot be infringed by the government. Such rights, for instance, include an individual's ownership of her home. This right, in the private-right-to-censor model, would be analogous to an individual's freedom to express political speech. Other property rights, however, can be regulated by the state. These pertain to activities that in turn can affect other people's freedoms. An employer's right to maintain his property in an unsafe manner can be regulated so as to prevent harms from occurring to those who are susceptible and vulnerable to his actions. Similarly, under the private-right-to-censor model, non-political speech can be regulated when it adversely affects the rights of listeners. To exempt the media from any regulation of its products would be to immunize a huge sector of the economy from legislative oversight. And how ironic it is that many pro-speech advocates oppose special privileges like tax exemptions for religious organizations, and yet vehemently support such privileges for the commercial institutions of Hollywood.

Even though economic rights no longer qualify as fundamental rights, economic interests can still justify speech regulations. The Securities and Exchange Commission, the Federal Trade Commission, the National Labor Relations Board, and the Office of the Register of Copyrights all promulgate or enforce rules restricting various types of speech. Consequently, if speech can be regulated for economic reasons, then it should be able to be regulated for the sake of empowering individual control over his or her communicative environment. Put another way: If the economy can be regulated for political reasons, and if speech can be regulated for economic reasons, then speech should also be capable of being regulated for political reasons. Or, from a different angle: Since most media entertainment speech is really an economic commodity, and since the courts have long held that economic interests can be regulated, then media entertainment speech should also be susceptible to regulation.[34] The primacy of the seller-consumer function of the modern media, as opposed to the informational function so often touted by members of the media, was highlighted by a series of actions by CBS in 2004. Though it immediately fired a producer who interrupted the popular "CSI" entertainment program with news of Yasser Arafat's death, it never fired Dan Rather for a far more egregious misjudgment—the use of forged documents in an investigative story on President Bush's National Guard service.

The marketplace model ignores the communitarian aspect of liberty. It ignores that part of classical democratic theory in which free speech coexisted with the need for civic virtue and the pursuit of the common good.[35] The proposed private-right-to-censor model, however, tries to reconcile the individualist and communitarian strains of liberty. It also seeks to take a more realistic view of the individual within the modern social communications process.

The media often argues that it is only responding to what the public wants, that it is the free desires of individuals that determine the content of media speech. But this claim ignores the manipulative effect that the media has on consumer preferences. Individuals do not choose in a social vacuum what music they listen to or what television programs they flip to. Their decisions and actions are shaped by the context of the media marketplace; the choice of television programs is determined not in the abstract, but by what is showing when the viewer plops down on the sofa. Consequently, the free-choice rights of viewers cannot be measured at the end-point, when they are merely taking what's available and what they've been programmed to take; those rights should be measured at an earlier point in time, at a point when people have a fuller capability to choose not just what they will watch but what will be offered them.

Constitutional considerations must focus on the "overall life situation of community members that dictates their self-perception."[36] Constitutional inquiry must focus on whether people are truly and freely embracing the media speech that is being given them, or whether they are simply acting as malleable consumers caught in the tractor-beam of media manipulation. Indeed, the entire academic area of communications studies is based on the researched conclusion that individual preferences change as they are exposed to media offerings. Hence, until there is a realistic chance to escape that exposure, the true preferences of an individual may not even be known.

Centuries of political theory have recognized that one of the biggest challenges of a democracy lies in the development of the character of its citizens. Underlying most every area of social policy is an attempt to induce persons to act virtuously, for in the long run, "the public interest depends on private virtue."[37] As Thomas Spragens observes, "a citizenry without public spirit, without self-restraint, and without intelligence accords ill with the demands of effective self-governance."[38] The First Amendment therefore should not be interpreted in ways that deny the community an ability to foster such civic virtue, nor should it be interpreted in ways that deny the individual the effective right to choose self-restraint. The truest freedom is when individuals can choose how to construct their lives so as to attain their most noble ideals, because true freedom requires the kind of culture necessary to preserve free societies from their own internal threats. What a paradox it is when individuals defend a purely libertarian view of freedom, even as they decry the sinking of modern society toward ever more decadent and irresponsible expressions of such a freedom. But a society that cannot conceive of freedom as anything other than uninhibited self-expression must logically conclude that all things should be permitted and that all values are relative. Pursued to its logical end, such a mentality will simply judge things good just because they have been chosen. It is inconceivable how, in the field of modern art, "the dung-studded Madonnas and the urine-soaked crucifixes and the sadomasochistic photographs can claim to be liberating us from limitations, yet in actuality be dehumanizing and desolating."[39]

*   *   *

In general, current First Amendment doctrines recognize only the single, increasingly obsolescent focus of the marketplace model, which continues to fuel an already oversupplied marketplace of speech. There is no consideration of the types of speech being produced, or the effects of that speech on listeners or on the health of democratic society. As William Galston writes, the "gravest vices of popular governments are the propensity to gratify short-term desires at the expense of long-term interests."[40] While the marketplace model further feeds this vice, the private-right-to-censor model seeks to give people and society the freedom and power to deny those short-term desires. And in this sense, the private-right-to-censor model promises to be even more self-liberating than the marketplace model. Free speech is crucial "less for its role in disseminating information than for its ability to cultivate individual habits of the mind, focusing most directly upon the intellectual makeup and character of society."[41] But free speech can only achieve this is if the entire communicative process is free, if individuals can react to speech as freely and effectively as they are able to initiate speech.

The critics are mistaken. People have not turned away from virtue; they simply have a very difficult time turning toward it. The modern media world gives them little power to even reject what in a moment of silence they would see as decadence. The First Amendment is about freedom, but freedom in all its aspects, including the freedom to choose denial and restraint. It also embraces the freedom of the democratic process to restrict forms of expression that bear no reasonable connection to the process of deliberative democracy— expressions deemed so inherently lacking in stature as to not be worth deliberating about.[42] How odd it is that schools, in the name of child development, can control the kinds of media speech to which children are exposed during a six-hour school day, and yet parents are largely helpless to control such speech during the other eighteen hours of that child's day.

Notes

1. Jacques Steinberg, "Self-Censorship in Broadcasting Seen as Rising," *New York Times*, October 4, 2004, A1.
2. Daniel Henninger, "F-Word Fight Isn't Over Fei, Fi, Fo or Fum," *Wall Street Journal*, April 23, 2004, A14.
3. Ibid.
4. Howard Kurtz, "Time Warner, on the Defensive for the Offensive," *Washington Post*, June 2, 1995, A1.

5. Michael Medved, "Hollywood's Three Big Lies," *Catholic Educator's Resource Center*, at www.catholiceducation.org/articles/arts/a10033.html.
6. Newt Gingrich, "We Can Thank Hollywood for Our Ugly-American Image," *L.A. Times*, January 21, 2003.
7. Henninger, "F-Word Fight Isn't Over," A14.
8. Robert H. Bork, *Slouching Towards Gomorrah* (New York: Regan Books, 1996), 147.
9. Bernard Weinraub, "Carol Burnett Says Sex Jokes Lag Far Behind Belly Laughs," *New York Times*, May 11, 2004.
10. Ibid.
11. *Davidson v. Time Warner*, 1997 U.S. Dist. LEXIS 21559, 70 (1997).
12. Steven Heyman, "Ideological Conflict and the First Amendment," 78 *Chicago-Kent Law Review* 531, 605 (2003).
13. Eminem, in the music video for "Kill You," from the album *The Marshall Mathers LP* (2000).
14. Alexander M. Bickel, *The Morality of Consent* (New Haven, CT: Yale University Press, 1975).
15. Bickel, *The Morality of Consent*, 75.
16. Stanley Brubaker, "In Praise of Censorship," *The Public Interest*, Winter 1994, 48.
17. Terry Galanoy, "And Now—This Timely Message," in *Coping With Television*, Joseph Littell, ed. (Evanston, IL: McDougal, Littel & Co., 1973), 199.
18. *Chaplinsky v. New Hampshire*, 315 U.S. 568, 572 (1942).
19. William A. Galston, "Liberal Virtues and the Formation of Civic Character," in *Seedbeds of Virtue*, Mary Ann Glendon and David Blankenhorn, eds. (New York: Madison Books, 1995), 55.
20. Roger Shattuck, "When Evil is Cool," *Atlantic Monthly*, January 1999, 74.
21. Stephen L. Carter, *Civility: Manners, Morals, and the Etiquette of Democracy* (New York: Basic Books, 1998), 161.
22. Stanley Ingber, "Rediscovering the Communal Worth of Individual Rights: The First Amendment in Institutional Contexts," 69 *Texas Law Review* 1, 28-29 (1990).
23. Jules Henry, *Culture Against Man* (New York: Random House, 1963), 65.
24. Stuart Ewen, *All Consuming Images* (New York: Basic Books, 1988), 245.
25. David Martin, *Romancing the Brand: The Power of Advertising and How to Use It* (New York: AMACOM, 1989), 9; Edward J. Whetmore, *Mediamerica: Form Content and Consequence of Mass Communications*, 4th ed. (Belmont, CA: Wadsworth Publishing Co., 1989), 279.
26. Leo Bogart, *Strategy In Advertising*, 2nd ed. (Lincolnwood, IL: NTC/Contemporary Publishing Company, 1990), 5-6.
27. Cass R. Sunstein, "Beyond the Republican Revival," 97 *Yale Law Journal* 1539, 1545 (1988).
28. Steven Gey, "The Case Against Postmodern Censorship Theory," 145 *University of Pennsylvania Law Review* 193, 276 (1996).
29. *Lochner v. New York*, 198 U.S. 45 (1905), overruled in *West Coast Hotel v. Parrish*, 300 U.S. 379 (1937).
30. Cass R. Sunstein, "Lochner's Legacy," 87 *Columbia Law Review* 873 (1987).
31. R. Randall Rainey, "The Public's Interest in Public Affairs Discourse, Democratic Governance, and Fairness in Broadcasting," 82 *Georgetown Law Journal* 269, 283 (1993).
32. G. Edward White, "The First Amendment Comes of Age," 95 *Michigan Law Review* 299, 309 (1996).
33. Cass R. Sunstein, "Free Speech Now," 59 *University of Chicago Law Review* 255, 277 (1992).

34. Jonathan Last, *The Big Picture* (New York: Random House, 2005) (demonstrating the commodity nature of contemporary media speech by pointing out that motion pictures increasingly serve as the catalyst for all the tag-along product sales, such as soundtracks, T-shirts, and popcorn).

35. Rainey, "The Public's Interest in Public Affairs Discourse," 319.

36. Stanley Ingber, "Rediscovering the Communal Worth of Individual Rights: The First Amendment in Institutional Contexts," 69 *Texas Law Review* 1, 52 (1990).

37. James Q. Wilson, "The Rediscovery of Character: Private Virtue and Public Policy," *Public Interest* 81 (1985), 16.

38. Thomas Spragens, Jr., "Reconstructing Liberal Theory: Reason and Liberal Culture," in *Liberals on Liberalism*, Alfonso J. Damico, ed. (Lanham, MD: Rowman & Littlefield, 1986), 43.

39. Carol Iannone, "Adonis Anyone?" *National Review*, September 3, 2001, 45.

40. William A. Galston, "Liberal Virtues and the Formation of Civic Character," in *Seedbeds of Virtue*, Mary Ann Glendon and David Blankenhorn, eds. (New York: Madison Books, 1995), 46.

41. Ingber, "Rediscovering the Communal Worth," 43.

42. White, "The First Amendment Comes of Age," 391.

Index